Plautus: *Mostellaria*

BLOOMSBURY ANCIENT COMEDY COMPANIONS

Series editors: C.W. Marshall & Niall W. Slater

The Bloomsbury Ancient Comedy Companions present accessible introductions to the surviving comedies from Greece and Rome. Each volume provides an overview of the play's themes and situates it in its historical and literary contexts, recognizing that each play was intended in the first instance for performance. Volumes will be helpful for students and scholars, providing an overview of previous scholarship and offering new interpretations of ancient comedy.

Aristophanes: Frogs, C.W. Marshall
Aristophanes: Peace, Ian C. Storey
Menander: Epitrepontes, Alan H. Sommerstein
Menander: Samia, Matthew Wright
Plautus: Casina, David Christenson
Plautus: Curculio, T. H. M. Gellar-Goad
Plautus: Menaechmi, V. Sophie Klein
Terence: Andria, Sander M. Goldberg

Plautus: *Mostellaria*

George Fredric Franko

BLOOMSBURY ACADEMIC
LONDON • NEW YORK • OXFORD • NEW DELHI • SYDNEY

BLOOMSBURY ACADEMIC
Bloomsbury Publishing Plc
50 Bedford Square, London, WC1B 3DP, UK
1385 Broadway, New York, NY 10018, USA
29 Earlsfort Terrace, Dublin 2, Ireland

BLOOMSBURY, BLOOMSBURY ACADEMIC and the Diana logo are trademarks of Bloomsbury Publishing Plc

First published in Great Britain 2022
This paperback edition published 2023

Cover design: Terry Woodley
Cover image © Comic Actor Seated on Altar, Roman, second century CE,
Bronze, 14.6cm, Wadsworth Atheneum Museum of Art, Hartford, CT,
Gift of J. Pierpont Morgan, 1917.886.
Photo: Allen Phillips/Wadsworth Atheneum

A catalogue record for this book is available from the British Library.

Library of Congress Cataloging-in-Publication Data
Names: Franko, George Fredric, author.
Title: Plautus : Mostellaria / George Fredric Franko.
Other titles: Bloomsbury ancient comedy companions.
Description: London : Bloomsbury Academic, 2022. | Series: Bloomsbury ancient comedy companions | Includes bibliographical references and index.
Identifiers: LCCN 2021027012 (print) | LCCN 2021027013 (ebook) |
ISBN 9781350188419 (hardback) | ISBN 9781350188426 (ebook) |
ISBN 9781350188433 (epub)
Subjects: LCSH: Plautus, Titus Maccius. Mostellaria. |
Latin drama (Comedy–History and criticism.
Classification: LCC PA6568.M73 F73 2022 (print) | LCC PA6568.M73 (ebook) |
DDC 872/.01—dc23
LC record available at https://lccn.loc.gov/2021027012
LC ebook record available at https://lccn.loc.gov/2021027013

ISBN: HB: 978-1-3501-8841-9
PB: 978-1-3502-0538-3
ePDF: 978-1-3501-8842-6
eBook: 978-1-3501-8843-3

Series: Bloomsbury Ancient Comedy Companions

Typeset by RefineCatch Limited, Bungay, Suffolk

To find out more about our authors and books visit www.bloomsbury.com and sign up for our newsletters.

Contents

Preface vii

Playbill ix

- Summary and Highlights ix
- Character Names and Meanings xiii
- Synopsis and Arcs xiv

1 Why Plautus? Why *Mostellaria*? 1

- Ghostly Greek Comic Ancestors 3
- Ghastly Roman Renovations? 6
- Translation, the *Odyssey*, and Versatile Plautus 11

2 Foundations and Frames 17

- Venue and Date 17
- Roman Slavery 19
- The Traffic in Women 27
- Expenses of Monstrous Scale 32
- Rural Roman Conservatism and Urban Greek Liberality 37
- Paratheatrical Performances and the Roman Forum 39
- Ghosts, Haunted Houses, and Superstition 47

3 Staging *Mostellaria* 53

- The Roman *Scaena* 53
- Masks, Characterization, and Actors 59
- Costumes and Props 64
- Embedded Stage Directions 66
- Monologues, Asides, and Eavesdropping 70
- Metatheater 76
- Improvisation 80
- Meter 83
- Farce and Low Resolution 90

4 Afterlife and Ghost Lights 93
The *Postmortem* Scripts 93
Three Early Modern English Reincarnations 97
A Funny Thing Happened on the Way to the Forum 106
Tranio Trickster 111

Appendix 1: Pliny's "Haunted House" 115
Appendix 2: A Doubling Chart 117
Appendix 3: Character Line Counts 119
Appendix 4: A Selective Chronology 121
Notes 123
Editions and English Translations 141
Works Cited 143
Index 155

Preface

D.M.

(*Dis Manibus*, to the Departed Shades of the Dead)

2020 was a horrific year for the world. Composing this companion amid isolation and uncertainty, I was conscious of the privilege I enjoyed as an individual on sabbatical with employment and health care assured. Working on a comedy named after a ghost during a pandemic infused my thinking with a gravity unforeseen but I hope helpful to readers.

I wish to thank the series editors Toph Marshall and Niall Slater for their kind invitation to contribute this companion. Their careful, rigorous criticism of the manuscript removed much of my foolishness, but no team could possibly find it all. Their offer came as a *hermaion*, a lucky strike at an opportune moment with the completion of *A Companion to Plautus* (a pleasure to co-edit with Dorota Dutsch), from whose contributors I learned much. Thanks also to Bloomsbury's insightful anonymous referees and the friendly, efficient people of their production team, including Georgie Leighton, Lily Mac Mahon, Rachel Walker, Merv Honeywood, and Paul King. Gratefully I acknowledge a debt owed to students, with whom I have explored the classical world in over forty different courses spanning nearly three decades at Hollins University, a small liberal arts college for women. Chapter 1 and parts of Chapter 4 are informed by courses on Greek and Latin literature, both in translation and the original languages; Chapter 2 by courses on both Greek and Roman history. Chapter 3 draws upon experiences co-directing plays of Plautus in Latin at the Virginia Governor's Latin Academy, a three-week intensive program for high school students. Co-directing *Mostellaria* with Daniel McCaffrey was a hoot, and the student actors working with only a dozen rehearsals totaling twenty-odd hours would have made Tranio proud with their improvisational abilities. Parts of Chapters 3 and 4 draw upon graduate study in Shakespeare and Performance at Mary Baldwin University in conjunction with the American Shakespeare Center. Warm thanks to Paul Menzer for his critique of Chapter 4, and special thanks to Daniel McCaffrey, Dorota Dutsch, and Donovan O'Daniel, who read and made perceptive comments on the entire manuscript.

Playbill

Summary and Highlights

Playbills routinely include a plot summary, which serves as both an advertisement and an aide-memoir. If you have not read or seen *Mostellaria*, I hope that the following sketch will pique your interest. If you already know the play, consider the following thousand words a refresher on the play's distinctive episodes. Either way, you probably know that a bare bones plot summary buries all the fun of farce.

Scene 1 opens with a slap and an abusive slanging match between the rustic slave Grumio and the urban slave Tranio, the star of the show. Grumio accuses Tranio of corrupting the young man Philolaches in the absence of his father Theopropides, who has been away on business in Egypt for three years. Tranio celebrates the prodigal, Greeky lifestyle of prostitutes, drinking parties, and gourmet dining. Both depart, Grumio to the farm and Tranio to shop for dinner.

Scene 2 features a long solo song by Philolaches that introduces the play's leitmotif of houses. Addressing the audience, he compares a youth to a house: after parents carefully lay a lad's moral foundation and edify him with education, neglect and storms of passion can demolish the structure. Love has ruined Philolaches.

Scene 3 introduces us to his beloved Philematium emerging from her bath. Philolaches purchased the freedom of this former sex laborer, and she now resides in his home along with her older attendant Scapha. As Philematium grooms, Philolaches makes comical (and creepy) asides to the audience praising Philematium and critiquing Scapha. This is Plautus' longest eavesdropping scene. It offers rich, complicated commentary on the precarious position of unmarried women in Roman comedy. Finally, Philolaches greets them and dismisses Scapha. The couple professes their mutual affection in financial terms before reclining in the street to drink.

Scene 4 treats us to boisterous carousing with the entry of a drunken Callidamates and his girlfriend Delphium. Song and dance enliven the impromptu symposium. After the two couples recline, Tranio bursts on stage with a tragic message: Theopropides is home! To save Philolaches, Tranio shoos the revelers inside the house, orders them to keep quiet, and double locks the door so that no one can enter or exit. Alone and locked outside the house, Tranio promises the audience that he will stage a comedy/funeral games for the old man.

Scene 5 introduces Theopropides, a superstitious, gullible, and theatrically obtuse old man. When he asks Tranio why his door is locked, Tranio improvises a tale that the household moved away months ago because the ghost of a man murdered for gold haunts the premises. *Mostellaria* (*The Little Ghost Play*) takes its name from this scene. By banging the door and calling to Tranio, the revelers inside nearly wreck his play-within-a-play at its outset:

Theopropides
Sh-sh!
Tranio
By Hercules, what happened?
Theopropides
The door creaked!
Tranio (*pointing to Theopropides*)
He knocked!
Theopropides
I don't have a drop of blood!
The dead summon me to Hades while I'm still alive!
Tranio (*aside to us*)
I'm dead! *Those* guys are gonna discombobulate this here play.
I'm terribly terrified *this* guy is gonna catch me red handed.
Theopropides
What are you saying to yourself?
Tranio
Get away from the door!
Run away! Please, by Hercules!

Theopropides

Where should I run to? You run too!

Tranio

I'm not terrified. I'm at peace with the dead.

Voice inside:

Yo! Tranio!

Tranio (*to "ghost" inside*)

You won't call me by name, if you're smart!
I did nothing wrong! And I didn't touch your door!
[line and a half lacuna in manuscripts]

Theopropides

What's troubling you, Tranio?
Who are you talking to?

Tranio

Oh, sorry, *you* called my name?
So help me gods, I was sure that dead man
sounded off because you knocked on the door!

506–21

The terrified Theopropides runs away. Victory is short lived, for one line later Misargyrides the moneylender enters to dun Philolaches for a huge debt. And ten lines later Theopropides returns, having heard the previous owner's denial of the murder story. At the play's epicenter, Tranio faces double trouble from the moneylender yelling and Theopropides simmering. Tranio invents his second extemporaneous trick: Philolaches is in debt because he bought a house … just next door! Investment in real estate appeals to Theopropides, who quickly promises to pay the moneylender tomorrow and asks to inspect his son's big purchase.

Scene 6 shifts our focus to the house next door. The merry neighbor Simo—Tranio's new target—emerges singing an upbeat song about his tasty lunch and avoiding sex with his wife. After joining Simo in a duet, Tranio lies to him that Theopropides would like to inspect his home as a model for architectural renovations.

Scene 7 begins with a short, slow duet in which Tranio convinces Theopropides that Simo has seller's remorse. Once again facing double trouble, Tranio unleashes metatheatrical jokes that critique the construction of Simo's house (and Plautus' play) and figure himself as a tricky crow deluding two vultures (Simo and Theopropides). Simo heads to the forum, Tranio and Theopropides inside to tour the house, and finally we get a breather.

Scene 8 feels like an interlude when Phaniscus sings a solo song about his role as Callidamates' good slave coming to fetch his owner. After almost thirty verses, his fellow-slave Pinacium arrives and generates a duet. Their arguing echoes Scene 1, and their banging on Theopropides' door shifts our attention back to the "haunted" house.

Scene 9 presents Theopropides elated with his son's purchase of Simo's house, and he sends Tranio to fetch Philolaches. But in Tranio's absence, Phaniscus and Pinacium reveal all of Philolaches' prodigality to an incredulous Theopropides.

Scene 10 confirms Theopropides' figurative funeral when Simo denies the sale of his house. Theopropides plots to punish Tranio with Simo's help. They exit into Simo's house, allowing us another breather before the finale.

Scene 11 begins with Tranio updating us that the revelers have vacated the house, and he knows that his time for trickery is running out. He catches sight of Theopropides plotting an ambush for him and maneuvers to take refuge atop an altar. From there he taunts Theopropides, who threatens to smoke him out. In this apparent stalemate, a now sober Callidamates returns to mediate like a *deus ex machina*. Tranio boasts that his deceptions surpass those of famous Greek comic playwrights. He receives a reprieve after promising to pay double for hijinks today and tomorrow, and Theopropides ends today's play with a slap.

Character Names and Meanings

In order of appearance:

Grumio, *Clod*
Tranio, *Tanner / Galley Slave / Revealer / Woodpecker*
Philolaches, *Luck-Lover*
Philematium, *Little Kiss*
Scapha, *Dinghy / Little Goblet*
Callidamates, *Beauty Killer / Lady Killer*
Delphium, *Little Dolphin*
Sphaerio, *Ball Boy*
Theopropides, *Son of the Prophet*
Misargyrides, *Son of Silver-Hater*
Simo, *Snub-Nosed / Monkey Man*
Phaniscus, *Little Torch / Revealer*
Pinacium, *Little Tablet*

Names in Plautus suggest personality or function in the story, thereby providing a target for actors. The meaning of Tranio's name is unclear and likely elicited different connotations for different members of a Roman audience. Possible derivations from Greek words include: "tanner's bench," i.e., a slave whose hide has been tanned by whipping (Sonnenschein 1907: 60); "rower's bench," i.e., a galley slave (López López 1991: 204); "piercer" or "revealer," which contrasts Tranio's acuity with the obtuse Theopropides; or an epithet of Hermes, the archetypal Olympian trickster (Fay 1903: 249–60). Staging and wordplay link Tranio to crows, woodpeckers, and a bird called the *bōmolochos* ("altar-lurker"). Aviary allusions make Tranio an ancestor of the mischievous cartoon magpies Heckle and Jeckle.

Synopsis and Arcs

This synopsis outlines *Mostellaria*'s arcs, scenes, and meters. Plautus structures his plays not in five acts but through scenes and metrical shifts. "Arcs" are units of action that begin with spoken iambs and end with musically accompanied trochees or mixed meters (see further pp. 88–90). Since this companion proceeds by topics rather than scene-by-scene, this synopsis also can serve as an index for locating discussions of a scene greater than a brief mention.

Arc 1: 1–408

Scene	Lines	Meter	Recap and discussions.
1	1–83	*ia*[6]	Grumio and Tranio argue. Pp. 19–23, 37–8, 67–8, 72.
2	84–156	mix	Philolaches' monody on the ruined house. Pp. 79, 85–6.
3a	157–247	*ia*[7]	Philematium grooms with Scapha; Philolaches eavesdrops. Pp. 28–31, 65, 79–80, 87, 95–6.
3b	248–312	*tr*[7]	continuation; Philolaches greets Philematium; Scapha leaves. Pp. 28–31, 79–80, 96–7.
4a	313–347	mix	Callidamates and Delphium arrive; party. Pp. 41–2, 63–4, 67–8.
4b	348–408	*tr*[7]	Tranio enters and ends the party. Pp. 63–4, 72, 78.

Arc 2: 409–746

Scene	Lines	Meter	Recap and discussions.
5a	409–531	*ia*[6]	Tranio tricks Theopropides: the ghost story. Pp. x–xi, 49–50, 64, 72–4, 77, 96.
5b	532–654	*ia*[6]	Misargyrides the moneylender. Pp. 35–6, 41, 74, 82.
5c	655–689	*ia*[6]	Tranio tricks Theopropides: Philolaches bought a house. Pp. 74–5.
6a	690–746	mix	Simo greets Tranio. Pp. 32, 86.

Arc 3: 747–992

Scene	Lines	Meter	Recap and discussions.
6b	747–782	ia^6	Tranio tricks Simo: Theopropides wants to renovate. Pp. 15–16, 75.
7a	783–804	mix	Tranio tricks Theopropides: Simo has seller's remorse. Pp. 87–8.
7b	805–857	tr^7	Tranio tricks Simo and Theopropides: a crow and two vultures. Pp. 16, 56, 75, 77, 95.
8a	858–884	mix	Phaniscus' monody on the good slave. P. 24.
8b	885–903	mix	Phaniscus and Pinacium duet. Pp. 24–5.
9a	904–932	tr^7	Tranio and Theopropides delighted with Simo's house. P. 75.
9b	933–992	tr^7	Phaniscus and Pinacium reveal all to Theopropides. Pp. 25, 45.

Arc 4: 993–1181

Scene	Lines	Meter	Recap and discussions.
10	993–1040	ia^6	Simo confirms the trickery to Theopropides. Pp. 45, 69.
11a	1041–1121	tr^7	Theopropides corners Tranio on the altar. Pp. 57–9, 75–6.
11b	1122–1181	tr^7	Callidamates mediates between Theopropides and Tranio. Pp. 57–9, 62–3, 92.

1

Why Plautus? Why *Mostellaria*?

Twenty-one comic scripts attributed to Titus Maccius Plautus (*c.* 254–184 BCE) are our earliest surviving works of Latin literature. Seniority alone merits Plautus a mention in the history of Western literature and theater, and several qualities in his drama continue to draw our attention: his Latin is briskly imaginative; his characters flamboyantly memorable; his staging infectiously playable. Plautus was Rome's most popular playwright, and drama figured prominently in the Romans' formulation of their national cultural consciousness. For example, according to the Roman narrative, Latin literature began with a play when in 240 BCE a certain Livius Andronicus staged a translation or adaptation of a Greek play during a public festival. Today, comedy in film, television, and theater is a multi-billion-dollar industry in the world's economy, and many of comedy's plotlines and character types descend directly or indirectly from Plautus.

Mostellaria (*The Little Ghost Play*) is one of Plautus' most breezy and amusing farces. The plot is ridiculously simple: when a father returns home after three years abroad, a clever slave named Tranio devises deceptions to conceal that the son has squandered a fortune partying with pals and purchasing his prized prostitute. Tranio convinces the gullible father that his house is haunted, that his son has purchased the neighbor's house, and that he must repay a moneylender for the housing loan. Plautus animates this skeletal plot with scenes of Tranio's slapstick abuse of a rustic slave, the young lover's maudlin song lamenting his prodigality, a woman's grooming scene (played by male actors), a drunken party, a flustered moneylender, a rakish neighbor, bold slaves rebuffing the father, and Tranio hoodwinking father and neighbor simultaneously. In many ways, *Mostellaria* offers a spirited introduction to the theater of Plautus.[1]

This companion aims to help readers and theater practitioners appreciate the script as both cultural document and performed comedy. To make coherent discussion out of *Mostellaria*'s sprawling farce, it proceeds by topics rather than scene-by-scene. Chapter 1 examines *Mostellaria*'s relationship with Greek and Italian antecedents and Plautus' status as a translator and adapter. Since the first two sections of this chapter speculate on shadowy evidence, some readers may prefer to jump *in medias res* with the comparison of *Mostellaria* and Homer's *Odyssey* (p. 11). Chapter 2 considers *Mostellaria* as a cultural document embodying Roman male ideologies about owners and enslaved persons; the traffic in women; the acquisition and abuse of wealth; tensions between city and country; stereotypes of Greeks; public performance of daily activities; funerals for and surveillance by deceased ancestors; ghosts and superstition. Some of those ideologies may fascinate and others may repulse, but scrutiny of them helps reveal the mentality of Roman audiences that Plautus aimed to entertain. Chapter 3 examines the play as comedy performed on a Roman stage with its celebration of metatheater, improvisation, and song. In *Mostellaria*'s farce, simplicity replaces complexity as Plautus aggrandizes his comic hero by stripping plot to the minimum and leaving Tranio to operate alone with no resources other than his wits. Chapter 4 looks briefly at the play's afterlife in three plays from early modern England (William Shakespeare's *The Taming of the Shrew*, Ben Jonson's *The Alchemist*, Thomas Heywood's *The English Traveller*) and the Broadway musical and film *A Funny Thing Happened on the Way to the Forum*. The companion concludes by positioning Tranio among some notable trickster figures beyond theater.

If the notes and bibliography seem a bit thick or wide-ranging, it is not to intimidate or be defensive; rather, I hope that interested readers can mine them for further inquiries and find a variety of approaches for digging into a Plautine script (with references emphasizing anglophone works). And since our topic is *The Little Ghost Play*, without too much apology this companion sometimes invokes ghosts and spirits as a metaphor.

Ghostly Greek Comic Ancestors

Many people approach Plautus as a font of Western comedy, an author near the beginning of a tradition and to whose works later authors respond. While Plautus' Latin diction is archaic compared to the later elegance of Cicero and Vergil, early does not equal primitive. Subsequent generations may retrospectively apply the label "archaic" to an earlier artist, but in his own context Plautus did not know that he was "archaic." He likely seemed on the cutting edge in his dramaturgy, for even when he exploited traditional elements he did so in new contexts and stylings. It remains important for assessing Plautus' creative achievement to understand that he did not compose his plays *ex nihilo*; rather, he translated and adapted foreign, Greek scripts for his Roman audiences by interlarding indigenous, Italian comic features. That understanding helps us to approach Plautus not only as a source of the comic tradition to be tapped by later authors but also as an innovative transmitter and transformer of divergent Greek and Roman comic traditions, one whose process of composition still has something to teach us about the creative regeneration of "classics."

We may think of Plautus as a kind of shifty necromancer, resurrecting Greek classics and reanimating them in a new Roman cultural matrix. In so doing, he participated in a Roman translation project of authors adopting and adapting Greek works and genres. Playwrights contemporary with Plautus composed not only comedies but also tragedies adapted from Greek scripts. His era produced an epic of Roman history that folded Latin poetic diction into Greek dactylic hexameter (the meter of Homeric epic). Latin prose emerged in political oratory and Greek-style histories of Rome in both Greek and Latin.[2] Thereafter, the appropriation and renovation of Greek literary forms continued to inspire most all Latin literature. We might think of Catullus recasting a poem of Sappho, Vergil's *Aeneid* refashioning Homer's *Iliad* and *Odyssey*, or Horace in *Ode* 3.30 boasting that his transformation of Greek lyric poetry makes him partially immortal.

Roman artists embraced the opportunities and challenges of this secondariness—of repurposing classics from Greek literary or visual arts—to showcase their own talents and visions. Motives for and appreciation of the Roman achievement has varied among individuals and eras. We can view their appropriation of Greek artistic culture as a kind of imperialism concomitant with Rome's military takeover of the Mediterranean; or a pragmatic opportunism in producing arts and entertainment to meet a market demand; or a marker of cultural cachet, much as serving a notable French wine when one's local vintage can be of worse, equal, or better quality. The Tudor translation project, wherein a torrent of translations and adaptations of Greek and Roman classics flooded the English market as England began to assert itself on the European political, religious, and artistic map, provides a rough but useful comparison.[3] We ourselves perpetuate aspects of the translation project begun by the Romans whenever we read or see translation or adaptation of another culture's art.

The prologues of several plays announce that Plautus has transformed a Greek script into a Roman play. For example, *Trinummus* informs us that "The name of this play in Greek is *The Treasure*; Philemon wrote it. Plautus spun a barbarian version (*Plautus vortit barbare*); he named it *Three Bitcoins*" (18–20). Not all Plautine scripts have prologues, nor do they all give such precise details. *Mostellaria* offers no prologue and summons us into the middle of the action, as if the play's ancestry held no importance. Perhaps surprisingly, thirty lines from the play's end Tranio boasts: "If you're a friend to Diphilus or Philemon, / Tell 'em by what scheme your slave tricked you: / You'll 've given 'em the best deceptions for comedies." (1149–51). Is this quip a kind of endnote to acknowledge Plautus' Greek models? Possibly. More importantly, whereas identifying the play's Greek ancestors in the prologue could imply that Plautus merely followed the trail of his forebearers, withholding an attribution until the end suggests that Plautus (or Tranio?) abandoned a well-trodden Greek path and broke fresh ground.

Diphilus, Philemon, and Menander were lauded as the three greatest Greek playwrights of the genre we call "New Comedy" (as opposed to the "Old Comedy" best represented by Aristophanes). The three were prolific playwrights competing roughly a century before Plautus. Sadly, from Menander's 108 plays we have only one complete script (*Dyscolus*), one nearly complete (*Samia*), and portions of others totaling perhaps 5 percent of his dramatic output.[4] Sadder still, of approximately 100 plays by Diphilus, we only know the titles of about sixty plays and have over 130 fragmentary quotations. From Philemon's ninety-seven plays we have only about sixty titles and 190 fragments.[5] Since we know that Philemon wrote a play entitled *Phasma* (*The Ghost*, Latin *monstrum*, hence *Mo[n]stellaria*), Plautus may invoke Philemon as a kind of curtain call to imply that *Mostellaria* borrows from his *Phasma*.[6] In naming his courtesans Delphium and Philematium, Plautus comes acoustically and alphabetically close to tarting up Diphilus and Philemon. Whatever the case, Tranio's taunting tone towards his master functions as a mouthpiece for declaring that an ironically servile Plautus surpasses his own Greek "masters." Diphilus and Philemon provided Plautus with the building blocks of excellent plots, but Plautus himself freely reconstructs and remodels them for Roman audiences.

Without the lost Greek scripts, it remains impossible to assess with precision the quality and quantity of Plautine alterations. We can, however, outline his usual procedures. In 1968, publication of a papyrus fragment with roughly 100 legible lines of Menander finally allowed direct comparison with a Plautine adaptation. Comparison mostly confirms the deductions of earlier scholars that while Plautus sometimes translated the Greek text almost word-for-word, at other times he made massive changes to Menander, as discussed in the next section. Nevertheless, the extent to which the comedy of Diphilus and Philemon resembled that of Menander remains an open question. Prologues reveal that Plautus adapted at least two of his surviving scripts from Diphilus (*Casina*, *Rudens*) and two from Philemon (*Mercator*, *Trinummus*), but trying to extrapolate the distinctive poetics of Diphilus and Philemon based mainly upon four complete Plautine adaptations remains speculative at best.[7] In short, the specters of Diphilus and

Philemon lurk just beyond our range of perception, their spirits invoked and indirectly felt more than directly observed.

Ghastly Roman Renovations?

For direct observation of how Plautus renovated Greek scripts, scholars have compared the 100 lines from Menander's *Dis Exapaton* (*The Double Deceiver*) with Plautus' *Bacchides* (*The Bacchis Sisters*). If we could imagine ourselves viewing the scenes in split screen, we would quickly observe at least a half dozen Plautine renovations. Those same renovations animate *Mostellaria.*

First, we would hear how Plautus changes the meter and adds musical accompaniment, transforming the dialogue of Menander's calmer, spoken iambs into more emotionally charged trochees enhanced by the *tibia*, a wind instrument. Musically enhanced trochees are the most common verse form in Plautus, and pervasive meter with music makes his comedy seem less naturalistic and more insistently, self-consciously (meta)theatrical. Second, the fragment of *Dis Exapaton* indicates an act division for a choral interlude. Plautus does not confine song and dance to interludes; instead, he intersperses songs, making his plays more akin to musical comedies. Third, Plautus' elimination of the choral interludes and act divisions in *Dis Exapaton* results in continuous, frenetic action. Watching *Bacchides*, we see a character leave the stage to transact business and return just five lines later claiming to have done it (525–30). Likewise in *Mostellaria*, we see Theopropides run offstage at line 528 and return just thirteen lines later claiming he met and conversed with his home's previous owner. Such blurring or collapsing of real time into stage time hurries everyone along, providing less opportunity for characters—and the audience—to pause and reflect. Fourth, by reworking *Dis Exapaton*'s scenes before and after the choral break, Plautus eliminates the father meeting the son. Plautus appears less interested in presenting fathers and sons onstage together in dialogues that could explore psychological interaction. Father and son never meet in *Mostellaria*. Fifth, a young man's soul-searching soliloquy in *Dis Exapaton* becomes in *Bacchides* a series of setups and punchlines, almost as if the character were doing stand-up comedy. Plautine characters step outside themselves to undercut sentiment with jokes and wordplay, making us aware of the actor behind the mask. Sixth, and perhaps most famously, Plautus amplifies the role of the clever slave. Although Menander's title *The Double Deceiver* does highlight the role of the clever slave, Plautus' trickster outdoes him by contriving three deceptions. The papyrus fragment reveals that the name of Menander's slave was "Syros" ("Syrian," a generic name for a slave from Syria). At *Bacchides* 649–50, Plautus' slave Chrysalus ("Goldoni" a highly individualized speaking name) claims to surpass Syruses who swindle smaller sums of money. Chrysalus invokes and disparages his Greek progenitor like Tranio-as-playwright mocks Diphilus and Philemon.

Many illuminating comparisons of *Dis Exapaton* and *Bacchides* have appeared in the last half century to corroborate the assessment of the first editor of the Menander fragment, E. W. Handley, that "Plautus likes his colours stronger, his staging more obvious, his comedy more comic."[8] The half dozen mutually reinforcing features outlined here—musically enhanced verses, songs integrated rather than confined to choral interludes, continuous action minimizing time for contemplation and maximizing pace, avoidance of scenes with empathetic familial interaction, slippage between character and actor, and dominance of clever slave—help fabricate the farcical features enlivening *Mostellaria*.

Such handling of Menander is not to everyone's taste. I say "ghastly" renovations because some later Roman literary critics condemned early Roman comedy, especially when comparing it to the Greek predecessors. Cicero (first century BCE), for example, claims that the roughhewn plays of Livius Andronicus were not worth a second reading (*Brutus* 71). The scholar Aulus Gellius (second century CE) complains that while he and his friends enjoy reading the scripts of Roman New Comedy, compared to the corresponding Greek scripts the Roman adaptations appear inept, lifeless, and debased (*Attic Nights* 2.23). But the judgments of Cicero, Gellius, and those who repeat them miss the bullseye, for they derive from *reading* the *scripts* rather than *seeing* the *plays.* They engage in literary criticism rather than performance criticism, and thus their analyses share the antitheatrical prejudice inherent in Aristotle's *Poetics.* Since Aristotle analyzes texts to concentrate on the poet's craft, his perceptive and influential study underrates spectacle (*opsis*), the extra-poetic elements of stage production. We should ponder how our very terminology can frame our discussions, such as saying "texts" versus "scripts," or "audiences" versus "spectators." Critical evaluation of a play as script differs from evaluation of a play in performance.

Plautus and his peers produced comedies for the stage rather than for the page. Consequently, we should resist unqualified repetition of Gellius' complaints that (e.g.) the Roman comic playwright Caecilius Statius failed to reproduce Menander's elegant and naturalistic dialogues appropriately because he "dragged in some other farcical/mime-based stuff" (2.23.12), and that Caecilius chose to be funny (*ridiculus*, 2.23.13) rather than naturalistic. Instead, we should make the effort of imagining Caecilius' script activated on a Roman stage and allow that comedy often prizes hilarity over—and even at the expense of—verisimilitude. In performance, where the more naturalistic humor in Menandrean comedy may elicit smiles, that "farcical stuff" in Caecilius, Plautus, and similar Roman comic playwrights may incite howls of laughter.[9] There is no contradiction in believing that Menander may be better for reading alone, Caecilius and Plautus for experiencing in a crowd. In renovating Greek scripts, the Roman playwrights' goal was never simple translation; it was recomposition with a goal of pleasing a different audience.

The title of this section reads "Roman" rather than "Plautine" because the fragments of contemporary Roman comic authors reveal a stylistic unity.[10] Plautus, active *c.* 210–184 BCE, may have been the first Latin poet to specialize in comic scripts, but a couple of poets had already established generic norms for Roman New Comedy. Livius Andronicus (first play in 240) and Naevius (*c.* 260–201; first play in 235) were older contemporaries. With only a half dozen extant lines, we have too little of Andronicus' comedies to say much. The roughly 110 fragments of Naevius' thirty or so comic scripts, ranging from single words to complete verses, reveal close similarities to Plautus in diction and characterization. Several titles suggest that Naevius may have been a bit bawdier, such as *Testicularia* (*Balls in Play!*) and *Triphallus* (*Biggus Dickus*), and some evidence indicates that he openly alluded to specific contemporary persons, something not dared by Plautus. Plautus' career overlapped with that of Ennius (239–169) and possibly also Caecilius Statius (*c.* 220–167). We have too little of Ennius' comedy for judgment. The roughly 280 verses from forty-two known titles of Caecilius offer just enough for fruitful speculation. Significantly, Gellius picked Caecilius as a fair representative for assessing the style and substance of all Roman comic playwrights, and in the forty-five verses that he quotes we can observe several Plautine elements, including bombast, bodily humor, and jokes with a kind of straight man rather than monologue.[11]

These early Latin comic authors were not native Romans and thus likely not native Latin speakers: Livius was a Greek from Tarentum; Naevius and Ennius Oscans from Capua and Rudiae, respectively; Caecilius probably a Gaul; and Plautus himself an Umbrian from Sarsina, if we trust a tradition supported by the pun at *Mostellaria* 770 discussed below. Located near the midpoint of a polyglot, multicultural Italian peninsula, the Romans adopted and adapted many practices from the Greeks, Etruscans, Oscans, and Umbrians, to name only a few of many, many neighbors. Ennius, for example, bragged of having three hearts because he could speak Greek, Oscan, and Latin. Ennius boasts of his multicultural core more than multilingual fluency: he has three *hearts* rather than three *tongues*. Roman culture generally and Latin literature particularly derive from an absorptive nature. So, for us seeking to understand the sum that is Plautus and Roman New Comedy, we need to consider the indigenous traditions of early Italian comic theater that he grew up watching and perhaps even performing.

While the sparse papyrological and archeological evidence of Greek New Comedy gives us something for analysis, we have almost no direct evidence for the key features of preliterary, perhaps even extemporaneous, Italian comic drama. We know very little of unscripted Atellan Farce, named after Atella, an Oscan-speaking town south of Rome. Those farces employed masked stock characters including Maccus the foolish clown (whose name provides Plautus' middle name Maccius); Pappus the foolish old man (rather like *Mostellaria*'s Theopropides); Bucco the foolish braggart; Dossennus the trickster and/or glutton. We do have snippets of scripted Atellan Farce from a century after Plautus, but it would be perilous to retroject the Latin literary evidence onto the Oscan preliterary forms.[12] Some may look to early modern Italian commedia dell'arte for analogues to Atellan Farce, but the comparison is at best vague and cannot be used as evidence.[13] Similarly, we know of mime—spoken or sung skits with musical accompaniment—in both preliterary forms and literary forms from a century after Plautus, but we have too little contemporary evidence for direct comparison. Significantly, the phrase of Gellius quoted earlier accused Caecilius of sullying Menander when he "dragged in some other farcical/mime-based stuff."[14]

Despite our lack of solid textual evidence, the impact of native Italian comic forms on Plautus seems clear. Since the drama of Plautus appears very different from the remains of his Greek ancestors but shares features with the remains of other authors of Roman New Comedy, we may conclude that the Roman authors incorporated inherited Italian traditions: Greek + Italian = Roman. Although the equation appears simple, we cannot algebraically solve for a singular Italian tradition by subtracting the Greek, because Italian includes a plurality of elements originating in Umbria, Capua, Etruria, Sicily, etc.[15] Moreover, we must factor in the available Roman and Italian resources both human (the training and talents of available actors) and physical (the theatrical spaces) to grasp how inherited traditions plus live realities could shape the composition of a script just as much as the mind of Plautus himself. Plautus emerges as a kind of Dr. Frankenstein, his monster being a mashup of Greek literary and Italian unscripted comedy, with his *modus operandi* being composition or recomposition rather than simple translation or adaptation.

Translation, the *Odyssey*, and Versatile Plautus

> What is translation? On a platter
> A poet's pale and glaring head,
> A parrot's screech, a monkey's chatter,
> And profanation of the dead.

So writes the formidable author Vladimir Nabokov in "On Translating Eugene Onegin." Even if we were to view translations of Diphilus, Philemon, and Menander as the heads of poets on a platter, Plautus was clearly more than a parrot repeating their words or a monkey imitating them.[16] The extent to which his conjuring of Greek plays constitutes commemoration or profanation is debatable. Since he wrote for the stage, Plautus aimed to reanimate their plays with living actors, and he did not simply revive their scripts, zombielike, with bodies performing in Greek; rather, he reanimated them by translating them into Latin for Roman actors and audiences. I would like to revisit the opening question of "Why Plautus, Why *Mostellaria*?" by situating our author and play within the phenomenon of Roman translation of Greek literature. To do so, I shall suggest that the Roman process of reception and renovation assimilates Plautine slaves to Odysseus and Plautus himself to Homer, as encapsulated in the concept of *vortere* (to turn).

We can expand our vision of *Mostellaria*'s ancestors beyond comic theater to consider other mythical and literary sources. Homer—as always for Greeks and Romans—lurks as a potential deep source or intertext, for his *Odyssey* provides an archetype for ghost stories, trickery, and a master's homecoming after a protracted absence. To be clear: I do not propose that *Mostellaria* explicitly invokes *Odyssey*, only that certain structures, characterization, and themes of Homer's *Odyssey* are good to think with in appreciating *Mostellaria* as comedy and Plautus as composer of dramatic poetry within the Roman translation project.

Mostellaria turns *Odyssey* upside-down.[17] Theopropides' home faces some of the same stresses as Odysseus': a *paterfamilias* absent for years; the resultant dissolution of a household; the uncertain time and means of restoration. But with Plautus we witness—and enjoy—trickery not from the heroic returning father alongside his son but from the slave of the profligate son against the returning father. *Mostellaria*'s opening scene transports us into a world resembling Ithaca without Odysseus. Two slaves argue over the economic collapse of the household and the moral collapse of the son in the father's absence. Rustic Grumio's longing for the return of his master and outrage at interlopers recalls the complaints of Eumaeus, Odysseus' loyal swineherd.[18] But beaten and spurned by Tranio, Grumio leaves the stage at line 83, never to return, and with him any advocate for rural conservative values. In the next scene, the son Philolaches likens his own corruption to a decaying house. When he meets his girlfriend Philematium, he vows that he would sell his own father to keep her solvent (229–30) and, in a most un-Telemachean remark, wishes his father were dead so that he could make her his heir (233–4).[19] Father Theopropides emerges as a gullible blockhead, an anti-Odysseus locked out of his own house. Whereas Theopropides rejoices to buy and move into a new house, Odysseus takes umbrage at the thought of his wife Penelope moving their marital bed. *Mostellaria* presents no wifely or maternal figure heroically defending the integrity of the home. Instead, we perceive echoes of faithful and prudent Penelope in Philematium, who revels with Philolaches and professes loyalty to him alone even as she courts the continuing attentions of other lovers (see below p. 31).

With control of the house as the focal point of the action, in broad terms both *Odyssey* and *Mostellaria* present love stories. Where *Odyssey* glorifies an older married couple enduring and overcoming obstacles to reunite after twenty years, *Mostellaria* celebrates young lovers seizing the days (and the nights) with financial and sexual extravagance in defiance of parental authority and stable marriage. Such pursuits are typical of Plautus. Romantic comedy generally aligns readers and audiences with young lovers against authority figures, casting as the obstacles older men such as fathers, soldiers, brothel-owners, rivals, and rulers. But whereas comedies by authors such as Menander and Shakespeare usually culminate with the promise of young citizen marriage and a stable household, Plautus revels in the non-marriage plot. Most of his plays do *not* aim for or end in a marriage; frequently, the Plautine happy ending consists of the young man's continued access to his mistress.[20] Since Philematium has been a sex worker, *Mostellaria* cannot end with a revelation that she is a chaste, wrongly enslaved citizen woman eligible for marriage.

Marital reunion is *Odyssey*'s super-objective, but much of the epic focuses our attention on wily Odysseus. Homer's narrative voice aligns us with the crafty war hero, the aristocratic homeowner returning to reunite with his exemplary wife and his son. That alignment also makes us complicit with Odysseus in his use of trickery and brute force. Although Homer makes clear that Odysseus' violent murder of the suitors and his brutal punishments of disloyal servants receives the divine authorization of Athena and Zeus, we can still feel some disquiet with the *deus ex machina* imposing a peremptory conclusion. *Mostellaria*, as lighthearted comedy rather than epic, aligns us with the revelers and elevates their crafty servile helper to the role of the hero. With a wedding not possible as culmination, Tranio's wiles steal the spotlight from the love story.[21] The wastrels become the focalizers, and we as spectators joining the action do not want restoration, at least for the moment, so that we can vicariously enjoy some of the fun.[22] Tranio's trickery poses no lasting threat to the established social order of the fictional Athens because he can only delay the inevitable restoration of a stable household. *Mostellaria* offers little sense of closure, for instead of watching a settlement between father and son we witness a hungover friend of Philolaches mediate for Tranio, who promises that he will resume his trickery tomorrow.[23] The ending suggests another opening instead of closure, for Theopropides' return has given Tranio a new target for his schemes.

The preeminence of Homer and Odysseus certainly were known to Plautus' Roman audiences. The fact that the first non-dramatic work of Latin literature appears to have been a translation of the *Odyssey* by Livius Andronicus demonstrates the prominence of Homer and Odysseus in Roman cultural consciousness. Latin literature's earliest authors embraced the Trojan War as the starting point for Roman prehistory.[24] Homer held such special prestige for Roman authors that in the opening of *Annales*, the first epic of Roman national history composed in hexameters, Ennius records a dream in which Homer reveals to him that he is Homer reincarnated. Ennius thereby claims to speak with the authority not of a pale head, parrot, or monkey, but of Homer himself.

Good fortune has preserved for us the brilliant first line of Andronicus' translation of *Odyssey*, which reads: "Narrate to me, Nymph, about the versatile hero . . ." (*Virum mihi, Camena, insece versutum*). This opening metapoetically celebrates Andronicus' role as conjurer of Homer. "*Mihi*" is not simply a translation of the original Greek "*moi*" (Homer or the reciter), for "*mihi*" also equals Andronicus, the translator and adapter who inserts himself into the poem under the auspices of Camena, a local Italian divinity.[25] The adjective *versutum* (also spelled *vorsutum*, "versatile") identifies Odysseus as the archetypal hero of trickery and tactics, including a mastery of language manifest in his abilities to tell lies that sound like the truth and to weave long, mesmerizing yarns. The character of Odysseus himself, not Homer as narrator, retells his incredible adventures to the Phaiakians in books 9–12 of *Odyssey*. By virtue of this lengthy embedded narration, heroic character and epic poet become linked. In a similar fashion, Andronicus' *versutum* fuses the versatility of Ulysses with the versification of Andronicus' version. Since *versutum* literally means "turned" or "translated," Andronicus boasts of translating Greek Odysseus into Roman Ulysses through diction and meter (the Latin Saturnian meter replaces Greek dactylic hexameter). "Narrate to me," Andronicus says, "the hero translated." *Vortere* became the standard term for Roman translation of Greek classics, as in *Plautus vortit barbare* from the prologue of *Trinummus* cited earlier. Plautus, following the lead of Andronicus, gives us seductive versions rather than faithful copies of Greek models.

Readers of the *Odyssey* perceive a common narrative voice linking Homer and Odysseus. Andronicus' translation enriches the picture by adding a second dimension, drawing conceptual links among the two poets and Odysseus/Ulysses through the term *versutus*. Plautus draws a similar picture, using *vorsutus* to link Ulysses with both Plautus as poet and his tricksters as characters. Clever slaves such as Chrysalus, Pseudolus, and others share a "symbolic kinship with Ulysses (Odysseus)—the archetypal *vorsutus* and chameleonic hero."[26] Sometimes Plautus makes the kinship explicit, as when Chrysalus boasts "I am Ulysses" (*Bacchides* 940), or when a dupe of Pseudolus marvels "that Pseudolus is a very clever dude, very *vorsutus*, very villainous; he has surpassed Ulysses and the Trojan trick" (*Pseudolus* 1243–4). Plautine tricksters, like the actors embodying them, are shapeshifters, *vorsipelles*, as Chrysalus boasts (*Bacchides* 658). They appear as a mouthpiece for Plautus himself by functioning as playwrights and poets, creators of fictions that reshape and redirect the action on stage.[27] Rather like a hub, *vortere* binds together a network of entities seemingly unconnected or only bound to an adjacent entity: Andronicus' version of Homer's *Odyssey*; versatile Odysseus/Ulysses; Plautus' versions of Greek plays; Plautus' subversive slave characters; the versatile actors playing multiple roles.[28]

We need not insist upon *Mostellaria*'s more ethereal connections with *Odyssey*. The point is that Plautus merits and invites reading as literature, and in even his most lighthearted farce we can detect sophisticated pronouncements on his activity as a Roman dramatic poet. Tranio's claim to surpass Diphilus and Philemon in composing tricky plots compels us to evaluate Plautine adaptations of Greek theatrical and literary culture as a continuation, appropriation, or mutilation of the Greek. Do we see *Mostellaria* as *homage*? vandalism? postmodern mashup? Some polyvalent jokes surrounding Simo's house demonstrate why deciding is difficult.

In describing the architecture of Simo's house, Plautus introduces a complicated metapoetic metaphor to praise his own Italian theatrical achievement. In **Scene 6b**, Tranio claims that Theopropides wishes to use Simo's house as a model for renovation.[29] When Tranio praises the house's *umbra* (shade from the hot sun), Simo denies that it has any *umbra*. *Umbra* can also mean "ghost," a sly joke for *The Little Ghost Play*'s audience. It also means "Umbrian element." In Tranio's quip *Sarsinatis ecqua est, si umbram non habes?* (770), Plautus generates three levels of meaning: "is there a lady of Sarsina, if you don't have any shade/ghost/Umbrian?" Architectural features establish that Simo's house is Greek in design. His denial that it contains any *umbra* implies a purely Greek building, with nothing Umbrian or Italian in its construction. Tranio's quip alters the resonance from the architectural to the theatrical. It summons for the audience an audible phantom of Sarsina's most famous playwright, Plautus.

Forty lines later in **Scene 7b**, Theopropides finds fault with Simo's doorposts. Tranio thinks them salvageable, if just coated with some pitch, for no "porridge-eating barbarian workman" (*pultiphagus opifex barbarus*, 828) made them. Plautus himself is that "barbarian" artisan, as in *Plautus vortit barbare*.[30] Tranio proceeds to mock the two old men in the doorway, claiming to see a painting wherein a crow taunts and plucks two vultures. Old Theopropides can see no such representational art. The image blatantly represents Tranio mocking Theopropides and Simo. More subtly, we may understand that upstart crow as Plautus, mocking the two older authors Diphilus and Philemon.

2

Foundations and Frames

Mostellaria can be enjoyed independent of historical context. Knowledge of contexts, however, enriches our understanding and appreciation of any artistic creation, and so this chapter investigates scenes in *Mostellaria* for features of Roman society obvious and immediate to Plautus' audiences but possibly obscure and remote to us. Although the setting is "Athens," *Mostellaria* addresses Roman social practices and tensions, or at least Greek practices comprehensible to the Romans, of which some are familiar, others strange, and a few repugnant to modern sensibilities. This chapter's relatively long and heavy analysis of two fundamental systems of power on which the play depends—slavery and the traffic in women—risks making the farce uncomfortable, less funny, or even unreadable and unwatchable to some. Yet these two topics tend to generate the most intense classroom discussions, and readers and theater practitioners should not gloss over the abhorrent bits or dismiss them with "well, things were different back then." Yes, they were; but useful perspectives emerge from pondering, for example, the reality that Roman spectators might relish comedies and the blood sport of gladiatorial games at the same funeral celebration.[1] This chapter is not an historical commentary on *Mostellaria* but an attempt to reconstruct key contextual foundations upon which this haunted house stands in order to empower readers with more interpretive frames and theater practitioners with more informed and playable choices.

Venue and Date

We do not know the precise venue and date of *Mostellaria*'s premiere, but several established practices are clear. Since Rome in Plautus' era lacked a permanent, purpose-built theater, dramatic performances shared the same physical and ideological spaces as Roman religious, political, legal, and commercial activities. That tradition differed significantly from the experience of classical Athenian drama, where the Theater of Dionysus was visually cut off from the civic center of Athens by the looming Acropolis (and even if it were not, the spectators faced away from the key buildings of Athenian democracy in the Agora, on the Areopagus, and the Pnyx). The plays of Plautus were a prominent feature of *ludi*, the public celebrations in honor of the gods funded by Roman magistrates that entailed a temporary, holiday takeover of civic spaces in the heart of Rome. The buildings essential to the daily exercise of Roman religion, politics, law, and commerce likely remained conspicuous throughout a performance. For example, a speech in *Curculio* (462–86) identifies landmarks of the Roman Forum visible to the play's spectators.[2] We do not know where *Mostellaria* was staged, and nothing in the play depends upon a specific venue for comprehension, but for some passages a staging in the Forum would offer the richest resonances. Whatever the case, while the *palliata*'s imaginary setting may be Athens, the real visual backdrop was always Rome.[3] That fact strengthens arguments for evaluating key elements of *Mostellaria* as a performance of Roman identities and practices, albeit channeled through a comedy derived from a Greek model, set in Greece, with characters dressed and supposedly behaving like Greeks.

Mostellaria is undated and undatable because Plautus does not sprinkle his plays with topical allusions to specific events and individuals in the way that, for example, Aristophanes does.[4] Indeed, Plautus' two plays for which we have externally attested dates provide no explicit internal evidence for those dates (*Stichus* 200 BCE; *Pseudolus* 191). Dating *Mostellaria* to 193 BCE or soon thereafter is plausible but not necessary.[5] Plautine topicality operates at the broad level of addressing generalized, fundamental, and enduring currents in Roman society. Although Roman society began to experience changes during Plautus' lifetime that would alter its structures and operations significantly, surveyors of Roman social history must be wary of telescoping developments that took centuries into decades, or decades into years. With a few notable exceptions, we do better to stress continuity over change. Put another way, the individual consuls changed annually, but the powers of the consulship remained constant for generations; the enemies and locations of wars changed, but warfare remained a central part of Roman life year after year; life's daily routines did not see the accelerated technological changes to which we are accustomed. We can with confidence take the active years of Plautus' career as a coherent historical period for our survey of the following topics.[6]

Roman Slavery

With no prologue, *Mostellaria*'s opening lines call out the star of the show, Tranio, and call us into a comic realm populated by enslaved persons. Since slavery was a fundamental and ubiquitous constituent of Roman society and Roman comedy, I would like to start by situating Plautus' play within that context. The verbal and physical abuse exchanged by Grumio and Tranio in **Scene 1** always gets laughs in performance but, upon reflection, could shock some modern sensibilities. Of course, the comic frame primes us to laugh and inoculates us against the sympathy or outrage that we would feel at witnessing real violence. As with, for example, *The Three Stooges*, the slapstick violence is choreographed rather than real. Moreover, the actors' masks mitigate sympathy or outrage by making them caricatures of humans, as with puppets or the animated cartoon violence of, for example, *The Simpsons*.[7] But even allowing for comic exaggeration, we might recoil at the sadistic tone introduced by the insult in *Mostellaria*'s first line, *mastigia* (from the Greek *mastix*, a whip, thus essentially "whipping boy"). Whipping of enslaved persons was so common a practice that Latin not only has a verb from the perspective of the abuser, *verberare* (to whip or beat, as in line 10), but also a separate verb from the perspective of the abused, *vapulare* (to suffer a whipping/beating, as in lines 240 and 246 when Philematium threatens to whip

Scapha). Grumio threatens Tranio with turning the millstone (17), the backbreaking work of grinding grain into flour often done by donkeys, implicitly dehumanizing him. Grumio also menaces him with iron shackles (19) and puncturing his flesh with goads while carrying a yoke or crossbeam for crucifixion (56–7). Crucifixion was a Roman rather than a Greek practice, indicating that Plautus shaped these excesses to resonate with the Roman experience of slavery.

We may smile at the hyperbolic verbal harm between co-slaves, but our sense of unease may increase with the mention or presence of slaveowners holding greater power to inflict physical harm. Later in the play, Phaniscus sings of his good behavior designed to avoid his owner's beatings (858–84). Theopropides claims that Simo has offered all his slaves for questioning in court (1087–8); since by Roman law slave testimony was admissible only under torture, those unnamed, unseen persons are imperiled though having done nothing wrong. Simo predicts that the returning Theopropides will whip, shackle, and crucify Tranio (742–3). At the finale, Theopropides indeed menaces Tranio with shackles, hanging, whipping, and death (1065, 1167–8, 1174). Tranio only escapes immediate punishment by taking refuge at an altar. Threats of physical abuse against enslaved persons pervade *Mostellaria* from start to finish. For some of us, those threats stand 2,000 years and an ocean away; for others, those threats are painfully close in time and space. What should we do with such "jokes" in Plautine comedy?[8]

Let us not sugar coat it: already in Plautus' era Rome was a slave society.[9] It is wrong, for example, to translate *servi* as "servants," as if these characters were voluntary domestic help at some Victorian mansion. Roman slaves were human property. In a chilling and oft quoted passage, the first-century BCE Roman scholar Varro reports that some thinkers classify agricultural instruments into two groups (humans; their tools), and others into three (articulate slaves; semi-articulate animals; inarticulate tools; *de Agricultura* 1.17). Such a mentality may underlie urbane Tranio's scorn for rustic Grumio.[10]

Those approaching Roman slavery for the first time must recognize two key differences from slave systems in the Americas. First, Roman slavery was not based on races or continents. Romans in the republic acquired enslaved persons from neighboring Italian and Mediterranean peoples, both indirectly by purchasing them through intermediaries and directly by conquering them with their citizen-soldiers. Totals for enslaved persons purchased in the Mediterranean market are unrecoverable, as are totals for persons born into slavery (children of slave mothers were slaves) and for the enslavement of unwanted infants. The figures for enslaved POWs recorded by Roman historians are spotty and may exaggerate, but from the Second Punic War to the death of Plautus the total reaches some 150,000 persons, which gives an idea of scale. The key point is this: "to a much greater extent than other slave-rich systems the Roman elite relied on their own military forces to procure a captive labour force."[11] Given high army mobilization rates in Plautus' era, a significant percentage of his male audience must have personally participated in the enslavement of POWs.[12]

Second, enslavement in Rome was not a permanent state. For many—though certainly not all—enslavement was a temporary condition into which one might fall or from which one might rise. Thus, it is often preferable to think of "enslaved persons" rather than "slaves" to emphasize the fluid status. Roman owners frequently freed their slaves, a process called manumission, and individuals freed according to correct legal form became Roman citizens. Slaves could save up money or materials (*peculium*, a distinctive Roman practice explicitly noted at *Mostellaria* 863 and 253) and thereby even purchase their freedom. And in a world unfamiliar with abolitionist ideas, both slaves and freedmen often acquired slaves themselves. Given constant Roman aggressive warfare and enslavement of victims, at the macro-level we may view enslavement as a process of assimilation and expansion of the Roman citizen body. At the micro-level we should contemplate Matthew Leigh's suggestion that "large numbers of Romans of the age of Plautus had experienced slavery from both sides."[13] What percentage from each group attended a play of Plautus is unanswerable.[14]

Leigh's observation offers a useful starting point for considering how Roman spectators could react differently to the Plautine portrayals and treatments of enslaved persons. Audiences were mixed groups with intersectional identities, including freeborn, freed, and enslaved; male and female; young and old; impoverished, wealthy, and middling; literate and illiterate; native Roman, non-Roman, and becoming-Roman. Such diversities and intersectional identities forbid positing a single, coherent audience response, even when a passage focuses upon a particular subgroup, as when Tranio seeks volunteers to suffer torture and crucifixion in his stead by calling out to the slaves and soldiers in the audience (354–9). Scholarly interpretations of the portrayal of slaves in Plautus have reached a wide range of conclusions based upon differences in their theoretical lenses, selections of plays or passages for emphasis, assessments of the impact of the Greek settings and Greek antecedents, and presumptions about the plays' primary target audience.[15] Moreover, we are dealing with comedy. Since no single theory can account for the various cognitive processes resulting in laughter, we should be cautious before accepting unscientific and reductionist interpretations—such as the conjectures of Freud, or that all comedy starts from anger—as a guide for understanding why various segments of ancient Roman audiences found the abuse of slaves funny.[16]

Returning to Scene 1, the clash between Grumio and Tranio is sometimes analyzed as a comic portrait of the "good slave" versus the "bad slave," as Grumio himself wonders (27). Such rubrics, while useful for exploring the script as drama, from a historical perspective risk imposing an oversimplified framework of stock character types and then interpreting behavior solely from the perspective of the dominant class. Since enslaved persons were human property, legally instruments for their owner's use with limited or no autonomy, how best could they serve simultaneously their owner's and their own interests in every moment? The two goals were often not coterminous and could pose dilemmas. Moreover, in Theopropides' absence the household lacks the usual clearly defined patriarchal surveillance, punishments, and rewards. So "good" in whose eyes? Members of the household must weigh loyalty and obedience to absent father versus loyalty and obedience to present son. Tranio must decide between reinforcing the whims of the son or enforcing discipline *in loco parentis*. Grumio's choice to avoid meeting and greeting Philolaches suggests a certain tension, fear, or alienation (82–3). Grumio pins his hopes on the father's return and pines for the resumption of a familiar system wherein slaves subordinate their personal desires to pursue rewards commensurate with their behavior, ranging from escaping a beating or demotion to gaining promotion or even manumission. We find here a confluence of drama and history if we put it in performance terms: whereas an enslaved person's objective varies from scene to scene, his or her super-objective is always to work away from a beating and towards freedom. Instead of choosing between a binary of "good" and "bad" behavior, Grumio, Tranio, and other slaves must navigate among the interests of self, fellow slaves, owners, and free members of their community.[17] Actors must choose among those navigable courses from scene to scene.

A conflict between rustic outsider and urban insider further complicates the simplistic binary of "good" versus "bad" slaves. Grumio is a cowherd working on Theopropides' farm. He seems to lack the authority of a *vilicus*, a farm manager holding the owner's confidence, as portrayed by Olympio in a similar opening scene of Plautus' *Casina*. Rural slaves, especially those working on a farm distant from their owners' surveillance, necessarily possessed some hard-earned autonomy in performance of their daily labors but were less likely to gain rewards, including manumission. Tranio's functions within the urban household are less clear. Although not a cook, he seems to have some oversight of provisions, for he emerges from the kitchen, goes to the port to buy fish for supper, and dispenses the cattle's fodder. He oversees other slaves (e.g., his commands to Sphaerio at 420). He also seems to have oversight of Philolaches, almost as a tutor.[18] Scene 1 establishes the degree of intimacy and license that he shares with Philolaches within the house: he lies beside him (43) and is allowed to booze and sleep with prostitutes (36; 22–3). Theopropides left him in charge (25), so presumably he had earned the old man's confidence to install him as majordomo.

With an argument between two slaves outside Theopropides' house, the staging of Scene 8 recalls the opening scene. Phaniscus enters first and, with the stage to himself, sings directly to the audience about the qualities that distinguish good and bad slaves (**Scene 8a**). The meter and content mark his monody as a distinctively Plautine composition, which invites us to interrogate his sentiments closely.[19] As Phaniscus has embraced the desires of his owner Callidamates, many of his claims espouse the dominant ideology: good slaves are useful to masters by promptly fulfilling duties out of fear; bad slaves run off, waste their *peculium*, and suffer beatings. One sentiment repays special consideration: "the owner's accustomed to be as his slaves want him to be: they're good, he's good; they're wicked, he's bad" (872–3). Enslaved persons such as nurses and tutors clearly exercised educative authority, and the corruption of impressionable young Philocrates by Tranio corroborates Phaniscus' claim. Phaniscus is not a tutor, but we may wonder about his role in the mixture of nobility and scurrility in his owner Callidamates. A slave's ability to shape a master's behavior could extend beyond adolescence, as when Tranio convinces Theopropides to show sensitivity to Simo's feelings and Theopropides thanks him for the good advice befitting a humane spirit (814). Phaniscus' claim suggests a general truth about a slave's influence within any household. Such comments remind us to approach Roman slavery, especially in urban settings, not as a legal or economic abstraction but as pervasive, fundamental, and intimate relationships between humans. The behaviors of owners and slaves were interdependent and mutually reinforcing.[20] Slave, freed, and freeborn dwelt under the same roof. Slaves were part of the Roman *familia*. Phaniscus' remark does not invert the power structure but reflects mutual acculturation.

Pinacium's arrival complicates our reception of Phaniscus (**Scene 8b**). Pinacium joins in the lyric duet but reframes Phaniscus' self-portrait. He taunts Phaniscus as a monkey, implying a thoughtless, subhuman mimicry of his master's behaviors. He calls him a "filthy parasite" (887), a stock comic moocher motivated by food, a charge that perhaps corroborates Grumio's earlier complaint that Tranio feeds parasites (24).[21] In the world outside the play, hunger and malnourishment were the most basic concerns of those forced to labor for sustenance rather than wages.[22] Pinacium brands Phaniscus as a counterfeiter of coins (892). The quip is both a metatheatrical complaint about recirculating stale, unfunny jokes in comic routines and a critique of Phaniscus' integrity, that he is not of the sterling quality his song would have us believe.[23] Pinacium sneers that their master Callidamates loves Phaniscus and uses him as a pillow, an object of (sexual) pleasure (890, 895). Within the play, the charge of passive intercourse with Callidamates aims to degrade Phaniscus, undercutting his credibility as arbiter of good and bad slaves. Beyond the play, we know that sexual abuse of slaves, especially the young, both male and female, was a vile reality of the Greek and Roman world. In performance, there may be something overtly carnal in Phaniscus' appearance and delivery, for after he addresses Theopropides, the old man remarks *puere, nimium delicatu's* (boy, you're too saucy, 947). *Delicatus* means "voluptuous," "effeminate," "wanton"; it surely applies to more than just a sassy remark, and it would render Phaniscus morally suspect.

Whether or not Phaniscus is Callidamates' catamite, we have little reason to embrace Pinacium's condemnation of him. Phaniscus clearly demonstrates more initiative, for he outpaced Pinacium by enough to sing and dance solo. In **Scene 9b**, Phaniscus takes charge in conversing with Theopropides and declaring it time to leave.[24] While Phaniscus may cite fear of beatings as his motivation to care for his master (992), one comment implies a hint of empathy beyond self-interest. After stating that Philolaches has effectively slain his father and denouncing Tranio as the most accursed and profligate slave, Phaniscus swears that he pitifully pities the pitiful father when he will find out (*misere miseret … misero*, 985–6). Perhaps it is simply cliché, or perhaps Phaniscus can extend concern for the welfare of his own master to others. A tendency to contrast complex, humane characterization in Menander and Terence versus stock caricatures in Plautus should not be pressed so relentlessly as to erase an occasional glimpse of compassion in Plautine utterances.

The constrained obedience of Grumio, Phaniscus, Pinacium, and Scapha magnifies the seemingly absolute freedom with which Tranio operates. Though enslaved, Tranio masterfully manipulates an environment nominally controlled by free people. Tranio exemplifies the stock comic clever slave, the *servus callidus*, whose preeminence is a hallmark not only of Plautus but of the entire genre.[25] The fourth-century CE grammarian Aelius Donatus comments casually on a line of Terence (*Eunuchus* 57) that: "in the *palliata* the comic poets are permitted to make the slaves smarter than their masters, a thing which is almost not allowed in the *togata*." Donatus may overgeneralize, but he had access to far more scripts than we do, enough to posit a fundamental distinction between the *togata* (comedy in Roman dress set in Italy) and the *palliata* (comedy in Greek dress set in Greece). Donatus' observation should restrain us from reading too much Roman social history into Tranio's portrayal and from seeing him, or any *servus callidus*, as either a reflection of Roman social history or a transcript of one group's ideology. The clever slave's triumphant audacity may reveal more about human freedom than about Roman slavery, as Ferdinand Stürner suggests.[26]

Enslaved status is not a requirement to fulfill the dramatic functions of comic trickster in the *palliata*, as demonstrated by the exploits of Plautus' freedman Curculio and Terence's parasite Phormio in the plays named after them. But Tranio's enslaved status is significant for two interrelated reasons. First, whereas Curculio and Phormio acknowledge the codes of social dependency and reciprocity shared among free or freedmen, a slave like Tranio who stands outside the moral networks of free individuals can more easily flout the "good" behaviors of the dominant class. To follow Stürner a step further, Tranio's servile trickery dramatizes "a basic conflict of societies relying on a foreign and unfree workforce: they are compelled to entrust important functions to persons who need not share the moral outlook and the behavioral code of their owners; in fact, they have good reasons not to do so."[27] Second, Tranio's enslaved status raises the stakes on his deceptions to a daring high wire act. Unlike free tricksters, if Tranio fails or abandons refuge at the altar, he could suffer physical torture before our very eyes. Imagine the play with (e.g.) Callidamates perpetrating Tranio's deceitful abuse of Theopropides' trust: there would be irreparable damage to Callidamates' standing in the community but no fear of physical violence. By contrast, Tranio has nothing to lose morally, everything to lose physically. And so we understand that *Mostellaria*'s violent opening lines are significant rather than gratuitous: threats and beatings epitomize the perilously high stakes that every enslaved person negotiated daily. The play begins with Tranio cuffing Grumio (*em*!, 9) and ends with Theopropides cuffing Tranio (*em*!, 1180).

The Traffic in Women

Perhaps unduly influenced by a search for the classical roots of later romantic comedies, many scholars (myself included) sometimes have summarized a stereotypical plot structure of New Comedy as: "boy meets girl, boy with help of clever slave gets girl." Such a tidy synopsis, while rightly marking the woman's adolescence, obscures the fact that generally the objects of the man's desire are objectified because unfree and unmarriageable. Most plays of Plautus strive to ensure a young man's access to recreational sex with a girlfriend rather than citizen marriage.[28] That feature becomes more disturbing when we stop to consider that frequently the "girlfriend" is a sex laborer. Be she free or enslaved, and her labor voluntary or involuntary, "only five . . . of Plautus's twenty-one comedies do not feature sex labor."[29] Peeling away the prim veneer of "romantic comedy," at the core of Plautine comedy we find coded dramatizations of the traffic in women. Beneath *Mostellaria*'s lighthearted farce lie daunting and disturbing questions about what happens after "boy gets girl."

Exploiting the fact that slaves are human property, *Mostellaria* equates the purchase of an enslaved woman with the purchase of a house. By noting this equivalency of person and property, we risk adopting the perspective of a purchaser and obscuring the distinction that the enslaved person has free will. Just as macroscopic examination of Roman slavery as an institution can overlook the myriad microscopic relationships between enslaved individuals and their owners, so, too, examination of a society's traffic in women can overlook the dilemmas and strategic responses of individual women trapped within the system.

Mostellaria gives us the lengthy and important **Scene 3** in which two female characters muse on their past, present, and future relations within a household controlled by males. Of course, being male actors performing in a comedy written by a male for a presumptively male audience, they do not provide a transcript of what contemporary Roman women were thinking. In addition, the scene reflects an unusual situation in the traffic in women because Philolaches has purchased Philematium's freedom rather than purchased her as his personal slave. She speaks under the guidance of Scapha with the increased autonomy of a manumitted person, and with it a new set of insecurities, obligations, and choices. An actor's choice of how to play Philematium depends upon the relative weighting of intertwining factors.

Philematium's past is somewhat opaque, and currently she occupies a precarious position within Theopropides' household even before the old man returns. Let us start with her profession. Rather late in the play, Phaniscus reveals that Philematium was a musician, a *tibia*-player (971–2). Female *tibia*-players performed at aristocratic male parties; their services included sex. Although we hear nothing of Philematium's previous owner, context makes clear that she was a *meretrix* (literally "she who earns money"), a term for which no single English translation fits but "sex laborer" is accurate. Characters identify her as Philolaches' *amica* (girlfriend, 538, 974, 1139, 1160). The same term is applied to Delphium (310, 311), and Grumio claims that the revelers buy and free *amicae* (23, plural). *Amica* is a frequent euphemism for prostitute in Plautus, and it does not necessarily evaluate emotional attachments. Additionally, Tranio (36) and Phaniscus (960) refer to hosting *scorta* (plural); *scortum* is a coarse term for prostitute (whore, literally "hide" or "skin," applied to both males and females). *Amica, meretrix*, and *scortum* in comedy reify "a hierarchy of politeness rather than of status," as Serena Witzke has demonstrated.[30] Plautus appears rather careful with the terminology: no one labels Philematium as a *meretrix* or *scortum*; she is always an *amica*. The other terms no longer fit because she is freed and no longer works for cash.

The experienced Scapha reminds Philematium of the provisions that an unmarried, non-citizen woman would need to survive. Scene 3 invites speculation by bringing out a mirror at line 248 (emphasized by a change of meter). The metallic mirror reflects Philematium's present appearance. Scapha serves as prophetic mirror to reflect her future livelihood.[31] The scene's dependency upon specifically Roman ideals for married women indicates that Plautus has departed from and greatly expanded upon whatever he may have found in his Greek model. For example, Scapha's remarks at lines 189, 200, and 226 cast compliance as the Roman wifely virtue of being *morigera* (obedient/devoted). When Scapha chides Philematium for serving a single lover more like a *matrona* (the lawful wife heading a household) than a *meretrix* (189–90), that polarity underscores Philematium's tenuous position as neither wife nor prostitute.[32] Freedwomen did marry their liberators in Rome, but we see no evidence that this couple envisions legal marriage. As *amica*, a concubine or live-in mistress, Philematium has neither the security afforded by law to a citizen wife nor the minimal protections of a temporary transactional arrangement. She has no male guardian and thus can be safe and secure in the house as Philolaches' *amica* only so long as he remains her *amicum* (195) and, ultimately, only with the approval of his father Theopropides.[33]

Although Philematium and Philolaches profess their love for each other now (303–5), Scapha knows from disappointing personal experience that a man's affections may prove temporary. She speaks to the precarious position of all women not permanently attached to a household in both New Comedy and reality:

> Learn reality from facts.
> You see what I am and what I was before.
> I, no less than you now, [lacuna] was loved.
> And to only one man I was obedient/devoted [*gessi morem*].

By Pollux, when this head turned gray with age,
he left and abandoned me. I believe the same thing will happen to you.
199–202

Scapha warns Philematium that showing the loyalty of a wife to one man is dangerous and advises her to play the role of dutiful matron only if she has a sufficient guarantee that Philolaches will provide her daily bread throughout her life (224–6).

Since Philolaches freed Philematium, a Roman spectator might suppose that she has one enduring hold on him: his obligations and reputation as her patron. In Rome, freed persons became clients to their former owner, their owner became their patron, and they shared an uneven yet reciprocal system of moral, legal, and financial obligations.[34] Philematium identifies Philolaches as her patron (167), and thus she owes him a freedwoman's gratitude, services, and obedience (205, 214). In return, he could be expected to provide certain protections to her as his dependent. But the allusion to Roman patronage inspires little confidence, for Plautus often invokes the patron–client relationship for laughs. He does so three times in *Mostellaria*: with Tranio to the audience (407–8), between Tranio and Simo (746), and, in an ironic inversion, Philolaches joking that he freed Philematium as his legal patron (244; a woman could not represent a man in court). Pragmatic Scapha looks to Philolaches only as the boyfriend (*amicus*, 195, 247), not the patron. No one presses the issue of his patronage.

Philematium is shrewd and not naïve. Scapha even describes her as tricky with terms often applied to the cunning slave: "indeed, by Pollux, I marvel that you—so crafty [*catam*], so clever [*doctam*], and so well raised—foolishly act the fool" (186–7). Philematium is no fool: she wanted her freedom (209–10), and to obtain it she successfully charmed/coaxed/fondled (*subblandiebar*, 220–1) Philolaches. She also acknowledges that other men do love her and will love her even more when they see her public display of devotion to repay her liberator (231–2). Eavesdropping Philolaches approves (233–4). In her precarious position, keeping her options open is prudent rather than a repudiation of love and loyalty. We find in Philematium's prudence shades of circumspect Penelope, who balances remaining faithful to her husband Odysseus and flirting with suitors. Philematium's maneuvering, for instance, recalls Penelope's appearance in *Odyssey* 18, when she showcases herself in the great hall and coaxes her suitors to elicit gifts. Penelope suggests that she might finally marry one: "Those who want to marry an excellent wife . . . give splendid presents" (18.276–9). Penelope's words delight the eavesdropping Odysseus, who stands by unrecognized as a beggar: "and much enduring Odysseus rejoiced that cunningly she was extracting gifts, charming their souls with winsome words but her mind pursued other things" (18.281–3). In performance, the objectives of both Penelope and Philematium are strategic, varied, and—to their male eavesdroppers—inscrutable.[35]

Philolaches' joking asides while eavesdropping on Philematium and Scapha throughout Scene 3 remind us that the women live under constant surveillance of the liberator. Scapha especially must watch her tongue carefully. She is Philematium's attendant, but Philolaches apparently holds a master's power of afflicting her with hunger, thirst, and cold (193, literally "killing" but presumably exaggerated). Scapha must balance her own best interests, framed within Philematium's interests, and encompassed by the whims of Philolaches. And Philolaches is not the only male monitoring the women. Philematium's outdoor grooming transforms spectators into voyeurs. Philolaches even directly addresses Roman men with dowered wives (280–1). By profession, Philematium is always "on stage" for an internal and external audience, and she seems proficient in performing love and loyalty to her liberator beneath an inescapable male gaze. The outdoor setting of Scene 3 demonstrates how her livelihood depends upon her expertise performing the role of *amica* in public and private, and the mirror presents her as an astute internal spectator, observing herself practicing that role.[36]

In contrast, we never see or hear directly from the one female securely established in her household: the neighbor Simo's wife. As an *uxor* (wife), she has no need to perform publicly her love and obedience the way that Philematium must. In **Scene 6a**, Simo enters singing with a mixture of delight after a delicious lunch and disdain at his wife's invitation for postprandial sex. His song reduces her to the comic caricature of the henpecking wife, more specifically the old *uxor dotata* or dowered wife. Roman comedy stereotypes the dowered wife as powerful, independent, and harsh, with the basis of her power being financial. Such a character brought a significant dowry into the marriage, maintains notional or actual control over that capital or property, and will take it with her in case of divorce. Although the character type derives from Greek New Comedy, its articulation in *Mostellaria* is Roman, with echoes in Roman reality.[37] Simo presumes a sympathetic Roman male audience for his direct address to those married to an *uxor dotata* (708–9). On the one hand, his absent and unnamed wife enjoys the shield of invisibility from the male gaze; on the other, she suffers the defenselessness of being ventriloquized. Above all, her phantom presence functions as a sketch of an anti-Philematium.[38]

Expenses of Monstrous Scale

Philolaches owes money because he bought a human being for pleasure rather than productive labor, and Tranio lies to Theopropides that the debt is for buying a house. Before we dismiss the play's premise as comic fantasy or a holdover from a Greek model, we should note some echoes in Roman reality from decades later. In 142 BCE, the noble Scipio Aemilianus lambasted a rival in terms recalling Philolaches' behavior: "you have squandered more money on a single whore [*scortum*] than the value you declared for the census for all the equipment of your Sabine estate . . . you have wasted more than a third of your patrimony and squandered it in vices." (Gellius, *Attic Nights* 6.11.9). Perhaps Scipio exaggerated, or perhaps he ridiculed his opponent by adducing a New Comic trope equating women, extravagance, and real estate. Or perhaps he tapped into jeremiads against the influx of Greek-style prodigality after the Third Macedonian War (171–168 BCE), when we hear that young men paid a talent for a boy toy and 300 drachmas for imported fish.[39] At least by the time of Scipio Aemilianus, public discourse saw such scale as scandalous but not incredible.

In Plautus, precise monetary figures are less important than scale. With the plays set in the Greek world, characters use Greek rather than Roman currency (1 talent equals 60 minae or 6,000 drachmas; *nummus* means a "coin" in general).[40] The value of ancient currency was understood in intrinsic precious metal content rather than a fiduciary or nominal value assigned by a government. Thus, characters speak of "silver" quite literally, as when Tranio urges paying the moneylender by bludgeoning his face with the silver (620–1; ouch!). Greek coins circulated throughout the Mediterranean, and any Roman merchant or soldier serving a campaign in southern Italy, Sicily, Greece, or elsewhere will have encountered silver drachmas. A moneychanger's knowledge is not necessary for an audience to grasp the monstrous magnitude of luxury in *Mostellaria*. We can never accurately translate ancient prices and wages into modern equivalents, but, given that a contemporary Roman legionary earned the equivalent of one-third drachma per day, the cost of freeing Philematium at 30 minae would suggest 9,000 days' pay, or over twenty-four years of infantry service. A price of 30 minae to purchase a courtesan is common enough in Greek New Comedy, and it is attested in the real historical case of Neaera in the 340s BCE (around the start of Philemon's career). While such a price would strain imagination for a Roman audience in the 340s, decades before Rome had even begun to mint silver coinage, the extravagant scale would not seem so incredible for Plautus' audience of the 190s and 180s.

Mostellaria's pervasive metaphors of accounting, such as Philolaches' oddly financial foreplay with Philematium to calculate their commodified love (297–309), reflect an emergent fascination with profit, investment, and coinage. Rome in Plautus' era was not yet a monetized economy, but it was transforming into one through the prodigious profits of imperialist expansion. The crises of the Second

Punic War and Hannibal's invasion had led to a collapse of the Roman economy, resulting in the need to create an entirely new currency system *c.* 212 BCE based on the silver *denarius* (literally "tenner," valued at ten bronze *asses*). The denarius system and subsequent military successes stabilized the economy, but recovery took time, even with Carthage paying large annual indemnities after the war ended in 201 and the silver mines in Spain generating massive revenues after they became Roman provinces in 197. Whether or not economic gain was a motive for Roman imperialism at the time, the fact is that continual aggressive warfare from Spain in the West to Syria in the East proved enormously profitable in bringing enslaved persons, moveable objects, precious metals, coins, and territory into the Italian economy.[41] Records of the booty paraded through Rome's city center in the triumphal celebrations of the 190s and 180s boggle the mind. Livy (39.6–7) specifically blames the triumph celebrated by Gn. Manlius Vulso in 187 BCE for the introduction of foreign (i.e., Asian Greek) luxury in Rome, including costly furniture, haute cuisine, and feasting with female musicians and dancers. Livy carefully documents the scale of the visible metallic plunder in Vulso's triumph: 200 gold crowns (twelve pounds each), 220,000 pounds of silver, 2,103 pounds of gold, 127,000 tetradrachms, 250 *cistophori* (silver coins), 16,320 gold coins. Monetary rewards of imperialism spread through the rank and file, as Vulso distributed double pay to his army, plus a bonus of 42 denarii to each legionary, 84 to each centurion, and 126 for each cavalryman. The period of 200–166 BCE witnessed a whopping forty-one triumphs (more than one per year), and the plunder associated with those victorious campaigns contributed to the transformation of the Roman economy. For spectators who beheld triumphal parades with regularity, the sums in *Mostellaria* would seem a plausible, albeit highfalutin, consumption of the profits of empire.

Young men in Plautus belong to households wealthy in real estate, slaves, and credit but short on cash. If we believe Grumio (81), his household's resources are now nearly exhausted, so *Mostellaria* opens at a moment of crisis. The entry of Misargyrides the Moneylender in

Scene 5b, the play's epicenter, embodies the crisis. The lack of liquidity has troubled families rich and poor throughout history, and so, while the scale of Philolaches' expenditures would have struck many Romans as extravagant, the anxiety of confronting bankers or moneylenders was all too real. Rome apparently suffered an acute credit crunch in 193 BCE, with the senate intervening to protect debtors from the exorbitant interest rates of moneylenders and passing legislation to curb some abuses.[42] Misargyrides' claim that he has never seen a worse year for lending (532–3) gains poignancy if *Mostellaria* premiered in the late 190s. Misargyrides is not called a banker (*argentarius*) but a *danista*, a Greek word denoting a short-term moneylender or loan shark. He loaned Philolaches 40 minae on credit, and he now tries to collect 44 minae (40 principal plus 4 interest; by insisting on receiving the interest first he will keep Philolaches on the hook). Philematium's freedom cost 30 minae, so Philolaches has lived high on the hog for years. Tranio repeatedly abuses Misargyrides as a beast, and such abuse is perfectly in line with prejudices against moneylending. For example, Cato the Elder opens his treatise on agriculture with a gratuitous attack on usury as dishonorable and the observation that Romans of old punished usurers twice as harshly as thieves.[43] In Cato's aristocratic ranking of occupations, farmers are best, merchants not without virtues, and usurers the worst. Through Grumio, Theopropides, and Misargyrides, *Mostellaria* gives audiences an unflatteringly comic glimpse of all three types.

Theopropides is a large-scale merchant (*mercator*) rather than a peddler. His entry addressing Neptune can be understood as standard thanksgiving for safe sea passage, or a literary nod to Ulysses escaping the god's wrath, or, if we press his allusion to credit with Neptune (437), an indicator that his business involves maritime trade. Whatever his exact business, he has spent three years in Egypt. While we must think away the luxurious stereotypes of Cleopatra's kingdom from 150 years later, Egypt did convey an image of economic opportunity for mobile inhabitants of the Mediterranean. In the centuries following Alexander the Great's conquest in 332 BCE and his foundation of Alexandria there, migrants from the Greek world poured into Egypt pursuing wealth as merchants, bureaucrats, bankers, mercenaries, rentiers, and middlemen. Romans in Plautus' era had far less interaction with and emigration to Egypt, but the country might connote an arid frontier offering rich economic rewards to those taking a risk, a sort of Eldorado on the Nile.[44] Theopropides evidently found financial success there, for he offers to pay his son's debt without hesitation, and something in his appearance suffices to satisfy Misargyrides with a five-word promise to pay tomorrow (653–4).

Very few Romans would have 40 minae available in cash for discretionary spending. Theopropides rejoices to hear that the sum is a down payment on a house costing 2 talents (120 minae), and he exclaims with pride that Philolaches takes after his father in business (*patrissat in mercatura*, 638–9). Theopropides bought their current house; they have no ancestral home and roots. Since he must have leased a residence for three years in Egypt as a metic (a resident alien; as a non-citizen he cannot have owned land), we might wonder how often he has moved or flipped houses and land as part of his business dealings.[45] *Mostellaria*'s plot depends upon moving into and out of houses in various states of repair and occupancy. Tranio's fib that his owner wishes to upgrade his house with extensive and expensive renovations (754–9) suggests an affluent and entrepreneurial sensibility that Simo readily believes. After marveling at Simo's house, especially the women's quarters (*gynaeceum*) and long portico, Theopropides assesses its value at more than 6 talents. The detailed descriptions of the houses and the architectural renovations could reflect tensions over the emergence of luxury buildings in downtown Rome as early as the time of Plautus. Theopropides' current house sounds comparatively simple, and, even with the play's Athenian setting, Simo's *gynaeceum* and portico "would have struck the Roman audience as conspicuously Hellenizing and exotic."[46] Dramaturgically, Theopropides' desire to own such a fancy house mirrors his son's desire for a fancy live-in companion. Historically, decades before Scipio Aemilianus expressed moral outrage at spending the value of an estate for a *scortum* in the passage quoted to begin this section, "Plautus portrays the house and the courtesan as competing objects of expenditure."[47]

Rural Roman Conservatism and Urban Greek Liberality

Theopropides owns a house in the city and a farm of indeterminate size in the country. That farm, while called a *villa* (68), should not be understood as a luxury estate or plantation. Although Grumio's threat that Tranio will soon work the mill and join the rural chain gang (17–19) might indicate awareness of large estates with their own mills, working the mills is a standard comic threat of harsh labor.[48] It is still too early to see in *Mostellaria* the transformation of Italian agriculture into the large estates worked by slaves that would precipitate the agrarian and political reforms of the Gracchi in the 130s and 120s BCE. But we can detect the beginnings of that transformation within a generation of Plautus in Cato's *de Agricultura* (written 160s BCE), with its strange patchwork of old-timey farmer's almanac and tips for cash-crop farming from slave labor.[49] *Mostellaria* offers no direct evidence that Theopropides is an absentee landlord exploiting large holdings of the Roman *ager publicus* (public land) with enslaved labor to produce items for export. Quite the opposite, for Grumio comes into town to ask Tranio for fodder (*ervum*, 62, perhaps here nutritious scraps from the kitchen garden?).

In **Scene 1**, the scuffle between Tranio and Grumio embodies tensions between city and country. Those tensions focus on lifestyle and morality, and they reflect both standard comic material and problems specific to Rome in Plautus' era. Tranio is an *urbanus scurra* (15). *Urbanus* is somewhat superfluous, for the insult *scurra* denotes a kind of city-slicker exhibiting elegance, buffoonery, and idleness. Grumio is a cowherd from the country that Tranio derides as country filth, a shitkicker reeking of garlic (39–41). Garlic concisely fuses multiple symbolic codes, including the olfactory, culinary, economic, geographic, and ethnic. Garlic stinks, imparts simple and pungent flavor, is cheap, homegrown, and typically Roman. In fact, Plautus' only direct reference to *Romani* insults them as reeking of garlic and leek (*Poenulus* 1313–14). By contrast, Tranio takes pride and pleasure in surrounding himself with symbols of a lifestyle antithetical to garlic. He enjoys fine smelling perfumes that likely are imported; he feasts upon gourmet dishes that must be purchased in the market (*opsonare*, 24, a Greek word for gourmet catering); the fowl and fish are plucked from air and sea rather than homegrown.[50] For an audience in the Forum, Tranio's exit to buy fish might suggest heading offstage towards the Tiber River or the *Macellum*, a market selling fish in or near the Forum to which Plautus sometimes refers.[51] But Plautus' choice to locate Tranio's quest for seafood specifically at the Piraeus (66), the bustling port of Athens, functions less as local coloring than a signifier of Tranio's enjoyment of a port full of activities foreign to agrarian Roman ideology.

Failing to find a noun symbolic of everything that is the opposite of (Roman) garlic, Grumio twice disparages Tranio's lifestyle with *pergraecari* (22,64), a verb Plautus coined to mean "behave thoroughly as a Greek" or "Greek it up." Phaniscus repeats the accusation (960). Since Plautus uses *pergraecari* in other plays (*Truculentus* 88 and the cognate *congraecare* at *Bacchides* 743), we cannot dismiss Grumio's slur as a one-off insult. Plautus returned to the verb because it resonated with contemporary Roman xenophobic prejudices. *Pergraecari* functions as a symbol or shorthand for all the seductive, newfangled profits of imperialism that led to the conspicuous consumption exhibited by Philolaches and Tranio. Grumio's checklist of their debaucheries at 22–4 ("drink day and night, Greek it up, buy girlfriends, free 'em, feed parasites, cater extravagantly") reads like a Roman critique of James Davidson's influential study of Greek appetites, *Courtesans and Fishcakes: The Consuming Passions of Classical Athens*. Within the world of a play portraying Greek characters in Athens, the concept of "Greeking it up" makes little sense. Since there are no Romans in the play, the Latin word *pergraecari* presupposes a Roman actor stepping outside of character to speak to a Roman audience. By scorning the slick frivolity and debauchery manifest by the other Greek characters on stage, Grumio (and the actor performing Grumio) seems to align himself with conservative Romans in the audience.

The ideology behind Grumio's metatheatrical quip cannot be boiled down to simple Roman ethnocentrism or to Philhellenism versus anti-Hellenism. As discussed in Chapter 1, the Romans appropriated Greek literary, dramatic, and artistic forms as vehicles for articulating their own national character. Through comparison and contrast, the Plautine staging of a Greek "other" implicitly draws upon—and advances—constructions of a Roman self. Plautus' contemporaries Cato and Ennius tout the virtues of *mos maiorum* (ancestral custom resistant to cultural changes) to offer direct and coherent constructions of the Roman self. In contrast, the multiplicity of characterizations in *Mostellaria* exploits emergent tensions between innovation, urbanity, and Hellenization against tradition, rusticity, and Roman *mos maiorum* without offering a singular, coherent agenda.

In assessing Plautus' presentation of Roman versus Greek, as with assessment of his presentation of slavery, the traffic in women, and economic opportunism, we must avoid the Intentional Fallacy. We cannot use selected passages to speculate on "Plautus's purpose," or to claim that "Plautus sends a striking message," or to propose that "Plautus's own sentiments may well receive expression here."[52] One cannot read the unperformed script of a play as one reads an ancient inscription. The playwright's purpose is unrecoverable and arguably irrelevant compared to the audience's response, and one must not champion the words of a single character within a play as the sole, authentic voice of the author's (or troupe's) sentiments.

Paratheatrical Performances and the Roman Forum

We perform our gender, class, occupation, and other identities daily. Romans—like us in a world with so many of our activities monitored, recorded, and broadcast—performed their social roles in a public eye. Theirs was a culture where divisions between the public and the private may seem porous or unfamiliar to most moderns. For example, we can view Philematium's grooming in Scene 3 not merely as a conventional theatrical invasion of the domestic sphere but as an indicator of the blurring of the public and the private, one that underscores her constant need to perform as *amica* beneath the gaze of her liberator Philolaches onstage and the Roman spectators offstage. Her fusion of public and private in a nominally domestic setting is not unusual. As Andrew Wallace-Hadrill observes, the structure and decoration of a Roman aristocrat's home reveals an "astonishingly public nature of domestic life" with an "interpenetration of the public and private life" sometimes incomprehensible to modern Western sensibilities. A Roman noble's house may even be understood as a theatrical venue, "a stage deliberately designed for the performance of social rituals."[53]

Moving outside the domestic sphere, a stroll through the Roman Forum or any civic center would invite observation of and participation in "paratheatrical" events, events that occur outside the bounds of formal theater but expect a person to perform a socially constructed role.[54] Some paratheatrical events were so extraordinary in time and space as to resemble formal theater (e.g., triumphal celebrations; *ludi*), others were daily routines (e.g., the interactions of patrons and clients; political and judicial oratory). All were in some sense scripted or choreographed by customary practice. Even with their Greek settings, the plays of Plautus allude to or imitate Roman paratheatrical events. Performing *Mostellaria* on a temporary stage in the heart of Rome collapses the distinctions between characters and actors, imaginary Greek setting and visible Roman surroundings. For example, when Simo exits the stage claiming to head to the Forum (853), a spectator's eyes might see the actor move towards real buildings a few meters offstage. Keeping in mind that the venues of Roman comedy temporarily appropriated public spaces of daily activity such as the Forum, I would like to focus on three of the many activities with a performative element embedded in *Mostellaria*: **dunning, dining,** and aristocratic **funerals.**

As discussed above, *Mostellaria* revolves around debt and disposable income, with a moneylender **dunning** at the midpoint of the play (**Scene 5b**). Misargyrides claims to work dawn to dusk in the Forum (534). That claim punctures the play's internal Athenian setting with reference to an external Roman reality, for the Forum was the commercial and financial heart of Rome. We know that bankers and moneylenders had shops on the Forum's north and south sides, perhaps within a literal stone's throw of the play's events on stage.[55] As a moneylender (*danista*) rather than a banker (*argentarius*), Misargyrides may be more mobile than sedentary in a brick-and-mortar office. Part of his hustle is to hunt down debtors, hence his appearance at Philolaches' front door. Misargyrides cannot take Philolaches to court or employ physical intimidation—mute actors accompanying him as muscle—against an aristocratic young man. Therefore, the moneylender resorts to dunning, public shaming by yelling out the deadbeat's name.[56] The tactic of dunning hastens resolution of the debt, even though Theopropides appears more concerned with why the money is owed than with any scandal. The scene offers a simple example of drama replicating or imitating a common paratheatrical performance. If *Mostellaria* was staged in the Roman Forum, the bodies of the actors recreated real Roman life in the appropriate setting, dissolving boundaries between the world inside and outside the play.

Then as now, **drinking and dining** *al fresco* is a kind of public performance. Normally a Roman would dine or sup within the home, later in the day, with some wine. *Mostellaria*'s onstage drinking party (**Scene 4a**) is transgressive for taking place in the open street, before midday, and apparently upon a whim to drink wine without any planned meal accompanying it.[57] Reclining on a couch with an *amica* to drink wine evokes the practice of reclining with a prostitute at a Greek symposium (literally "drinking together") rather than a Roman meal. Figure 1, a first-century CE wall painting from Pompeii, captures the scene's atmosphere nicely. The boisterous arrival of Callidamates amidst what he himself calls a *comissatio*, a drunken carousal in the streets, recalls Greek rather than Roman drinking habits.[58] Even if the scene

Figure 1 Fresco, east wall of the triclinium of the Casa dei Casti Amanti (IX.12.6), Pompeii, first century CE, upon authorization of the Ministry of Culture—Archaeological Park of Pompeii, further reproduction or duplication by any means prohibited.

exhibits an extravagant Greek exoticism, it still would be comprehensible and familiar to Roman spectators, and it serves to demonstrate the metaphor of Philolaches and company consuming his patrimony.

The concept of conspicuous consumption becomes most literal through dining. Grumio accuses Tranio of squandering—literally "devouring" (12)—the estate of Theopropides. The image is not uncommon; for example, the late antique scholar Macrobius preserves Cato's joke about a prodigal man devouring his estate like barbequed sacrificial meat (*Saturnalia* 2.2.4). The trope of devouring one's inheritance by cavorting with prostitutes and killing the fatted calf famously appears in the Gospel parable of the prodigal son (Luke 15:30).[59] The trope began to resonate in early second-century BCE Rome. Passage of the *lex Orchia* of 182 BCE, Rome's earliest sumptuary law on dining, reveals emergent anxieties over the displays of luxury in expenditures, menus, and the number of guests at dinner. A Roman orator speaking on the sumptuary *lex Fannia* of 161 BCE decries men anointed with oils and playing dice with *scorta*, drunk on wine, and stuffed with thrushes and fish (Macrobius, *Saturnalia* 3.16). The similarities to *Mostellaria*'s party suggest the intrusion of New Comedy into Roman political oratory.

Public surveillance was tasked with monitoring paratheatrical displays of private luxury. Macrobius, writing about Roman gluttony and the legislation to curb it, records that "it began to be mandated that people lunch and dine with their doors open, so that with the eyes of their fellow citizens made witnesses there be a limit on their luxury" (*Saturnalia* 3.17.2).[60] Rather than evaluating *Mostellaria*'s onstage drinking party solely in theatrical terms as a breach of naturalism imposed by New Comedy's convention of outdoor scenes, we should also evaluate it in historical terms as a document in rising tensions between ostentatious display and public surveillance to check luxurious gastronomy.

Although *Mostellaria*'s onstage party does embody a transhistorical, carnivalesque holiday spirit, within that general spirit lurk some behaviors specific to Roman *ludi*.[61] *Ludi* included rituals and traditions associated with drinking and dining. Gellius (*Attic Nights* 2.24) attributes the passage of sumptuary laws to curtail extravagant banqueting by aristocrats at the *ludi Plebeii*, *ludi Romani*, and *ludi Megalenses*, as well as the Saturnalia. The laws may have been more symbolic than enforced, but they demonstrate political attention to public banqueting in religious contexts. Venues for *ludi* with plays included plazas before temples, using temple steps for seating.[62] Thus, religious and theatrical activities shared temporal and spatial overlap, with some scenes in Plautus parodying religious rituals.[63] *Mostellaria*'s carousing on couches in the street perhaps presented an onstage tableau replicating human and divine paratheatrical activities in the same area. If so, some details may have struck spectators as mimicking banquets associated with the here and now of Roman *ludi* as much as exotic Greek symposia.

Mostellaria's party could have mirrored two paratheatrical banquets associated with *ludi* featuring plays: *lectisternia* and *epula*. *Lectisternia* were rituals in which statues of the gods were displayed reclining on couches in the street, sometimes with male and female Olympians paired on a couch, with tables of food set before them as if feasting. Livy notes the ritual in conjunction with festivals, including the *ludi Romani* and the *ludi Megalenses*. Banquets both public and private accompanied the ritual, such as for the inaugural *lectisternium* in 399 BCE, in which the doors and courtyards of private homes were thrown open in hospitality to all.[64] An *epulum* is a feast, sometimes denoting a specific religious celebration, such as the *epulum Iovis* given for Jupiter on account of the *ludi Plebeii*. Livy details the public nature of several notable *epula* associated with *ludi*, such as the inaugural *ludi Apollinares* of 212 BCE, in which people banqueted with open doors and courtyards (25.12.15). The funeral *ludi* of T. Quinctius Flamininus in 174 BCE included plays, seventy-four gladiators, an *epulum*, and distribution of meat (41.28.11).[65] Plautus' own *Trinummus* speaks of rich men and their clients reclining together at a temple banquet with choice provisions (*epulae*, 468–63). The convivial scene in *Mostellaria* could parody an *epulum* or *lectisternium* from an adjacent temple precinct, with the actor-characters replicating paratheatrical activities that happened the day before, day after, or day of their performance.

Mostellaria may not have been presented at one of the annual religious celebrations with plays (*ludi scaenici*) scheduled on the Roman calendar. Aristocratic **funeral** celebrations (*ludi funebres*) offered unforeseen opportunities for dramatic performances. Tranio's proposal to stage *ludi* for the still-living Theopropides that he will not receive when dead (427–8) establishes a thematic connection with funerals, even if *The Little Ghost Play* was not originally produced in conjunction with an aristocrat's funeral *ludi*. The verbs *ludere* and *deludere* mean to play, trick, or mock; the plural noun *ludi* denotes jokes and tricks, as well as holiday celebrations. After Theopropides recognizes Tranio's deceptions, *Mostellaria*'s final 150 lines bombard us with eleven forms of *ludi*/*ludere*, a frequency unparalleled in Plautus. Clearly some of those citations are puns, but the accumulation of forms seems calculated to demonstrate a fulfillment of Tranio's proposal to arrange *ludi funebres* for Theopropides.[66]

When first terrified by Tranio's ghost story, Theopropides exclaims that the dead are carrying him to the underworld while still alive (509). The play's subsequent clusters of invocations of death and ghosts reanimate moribund metaphors with meanings beyond the cliché and cast Theopropides as a dead man walking. In **Scene 9b**, Phaniscus reveals Philolaches' prodigality and Tranio's deceit. When Theopropides laments that Phaniscus is killing him (*perdis*), Phaniscus corrects him that Philolaches kills his father (*patrem perdidit*), and Theopropides concurs (979–80). As Phaniscus and Pinacium depart at the opening of **Scene 10,** Theopropides exclaims to the audience that he has died (*perii*, 993). He bemoans that he has returned from Egypt (a land of the dead mythologically) and now is carried to the farthest shores (994–5). Simo overhears him. When Theopropides asks Simo if anything new has come to pass in the Forum by using a technical phrase applicable to a funerary procession (999), Simo replies that he has seen a corpse being carried out for burial. Theopropides scoffs, but Simo repeats that this funeral procession is novel because the man was alive just now. Theopropides angrily threatens him, which suggests a bit of stage business to make clear that Simo has marked Theopropides as the corpse (1000–2). After Simo confirms Tranio's trickery, Theopropides repeatedly exclaims that he is dead (*disperii* ... *perii, interii*, 1030–1). The idiomatic *perii* (I'm dead/I'm a goner) has become leitmotif to support theme.[67]

Funeral processions of eminent Romans would pass through the Forum, culminating with a eulogy and pageant on the Rostra, wherein actors would wear wax masks of ancestors and a mime would impersonate the deceased. In an excursus on Roman customs, the Greek historian Polybius (second century BCE) outlines contemporary aristocratic funerary practices. He records that nobles kept masks of their ancestors in small wooden shrines in the most conspicuous part of their homes:

> This image is a mask elaborated for extraordinary likeness [to the deceased] both in the modeling and the complexion. During public sacrifices, they display these images and decorate them lavishly; and when any distinguished member of the family dies they take them to the funeral procession, putting them on men who seem most like [the deceased] in stature and general form.
>
> 6.53.5–6

These masked individuals, wearing the togas and insignia appropriate to the ancestors' achievements, rode in chariots through the Forum. They then sat in magistrates' chairs upon the Rostra, as if alive, as an audience for the eulogy.

An excerpt from Diodorus Siculus (first century BCE) on the funeral of L. Aemilius Paullus in 160 BCE corroborates much of Polybius' account. Diodorus adds that trained actors impersonated the deceased:

> Among the Romans, those preeminent in their noble birth and glory of their ancestors are portrayed after their death in accordance with the likeness of their [facial] features and with the whole general form of their bodies. They use actors who have closely watched his bearing and the detailed idiosyncrasies of his appearance throughout his entire life. And in the same way, each of the ancestors processes, having such dress and insignia of office that the spectators can know from their appearance how far each one had advanced in rank and shared in the honors of the state.
>
> 31.25.2

With musical accompaniment, the entire paratheatrical pageant must have been visually and aurally arresting. Dionysius of Halicarnassus (first century BCE) claims that he himself witnessed bands of dancers impersonating satyrs at the funerals of illustrious Romans (7.72.12).

Far from being somber "[t]he tone of different parts of the funeral procession apparently varied markedly from patriotic and solemn, to sad, to joyous and festive."[68]

We can scrutinize the foregoing Greek accounts supplemented by others for gaps and inconsistencies, but the general picture is clear. A Roman aristocratic funeral in the Forum was all highly choreographed, all highly paratheatrical.[69] We would not be wrong to describe it in purely theatrical terms: a pageant in which masked actors, in costumes, with props, accompanied by music, performed their roles on a stage in the Forum. If some Romans told you that they witnessed ritual *ludi* in the Forum with impersonations by masked actors, you might well ask if they had attended a comedy of Plautus or a funeral. Or one and the same. Plautus himself toys with the reliance of both *ludi scaenici* and *funebres* upon masked actors in his *Amphitruo*, when the slave Sosia beholds Mercury in an identical mask and impersonating him like an actor at his funeral: "this guy's got hold of my entire *imago* [likeness/funeral mask], as it had been before. What no one will ever do for me when I'm dead is happening to me while I'm alive!" (458–9).[70] Sosia's outburst approximates Tranio's joke to stage funeral *ludi* for Theopropides while still alive. If we combine Tranio's joke with Theopropides' exclamation that the dead drag him to the underworld still living, plus Simo's quip that he saw the funeral procession of a man, we begin to grasp *Mostellaria*'s pattern of introducing the funereal into the theatrical, inverting the usual encrustation of the theatrical within the funereal.

Ghosts, Haunted Houses, and Superstition

After the funeral, burial of corpse or its cremated ashes followed, with due rites to ensure repose of the deceased's spirit. Romans generally assigned an undifferentiated collectivity to the spirits of the dead, referring to them as the *Manes* or *Di Manes* (divine shades, often abbreviated on tombstones as *D.M.* in the dative case, *dis Manibus*, "to the divine shades"), but they could also distinguish an individual's *Manes*.[71] An individual's *Manes* could appear in various ghostly forms (*umbra*, *imago*).

The Parentalia and Lemuria were two annual festivals focused on interfacing with the *Manes*. Ovid's poem about the Roman calendar (*Fasti*; 8 CE) is our most complete source for origins and practices of the rituals, but it is not a dogmatic handbook. During the nine-day Parentalia of February 13 to 21, families commemorated dead kin at tombs and placated ancestral *Manes* with offerings of food.[72] Ovid relates that, long ago, a failure to do so led to ghosts wandering about howling (*Fasti* 2.533–616).[73] According to Ovid, Romulus himself established the Lemuria to appease the restless *umbra* of Remus, who had been murdered by Celer. The festival of three nonconsecutive nights on May 9, 11, 13 included an apotropaic midnight ritual by which the head of the household drove from the home restless, potentially malevolent ghosts (variously called *Lemures*, *larvae*, *Manes*, or *umbrae*). Most likely they were spirits of people who died before their time or by violence (*Fasti* 5.419–92).[74] Plautus' Roman audiences for *The Little Ghost Play* would have annual acquaintance with the Lemuria's rituals to protect the home and family by exorcizing ghosts of those suffering premature or violent deaths.

Scattered accounts from Greece and Rome report that restless dead sometimes could intrude upon the realm of the living as ghosts. Whether they be embodied or phantasms or dreams, ghosts arose from four basic kinds of death: before marriage; before one's time; by violence; with lack of proper burial.[75] Sometimes the dead could not rest in peace from multiple causes, as with *Mostellaria*'s Diapontius, who Tranio with exquisite overkill states died prematurely, murdered, and improperly buried (500–2). Modern analysis may impose a taxonomy of ghosts, such as embodied revenants versus disembodied apparitions; dreamed versus visible while awake; summoned by necromancy versus unbidden; experienced by an individual versus multiple people; true versus false; etc. But the ancient popular and literary usages upon which Tranio draws resist rigid classifications and treat specific distinctions as less significant than generic commonalities. We might here recall the mysterious ending of Vergil's *Aeneid* 6, with its underworld gates of horn and ivory. Through the horn exit is given to true shades (*veris umbris*) and through the ivory the *Manes* emit false dreams. Vergil makes a distinction, but we as listeners in the moment understand both as infernal emanations.

Like a poet, Tranio crafts lies that resemble the truth. His improvised ghost story (**Scene 5a**) would not have been at all credible to Theopropides if some aspects of it did not resonate with other Greek and Roman narratives about hauntings.[76] Among the many varieties of what we would classify as ghost stories, the subset of "haunting" most strictly denotes the spirit of the deceased lurking about an area, as in a haunted house, necropolis, or battlefield. Given all of antiquity's terminology, allusions, magic spells, inscriptions, images, and objects pertaining to the spirits of the dead, it is perhaps surprising that barely a handful of "haunted house" stories have survived for us in writing. From centuries after *Mostellaria*, we have a letter of Pliny the Younger (*c.* 100 CE; Appendix 1), two narratives in a dialogue of Lucian (second century CE), and a couple of Christian anecdotes from the fifth and sixth centuries.[77] The limited number of such stories makes it perilous to impose a checklist of typical or necessary elements, nor should we retroject strictures for our post-nineteenth-century genre of haunted house stories onto Tranio's extemporaneous yarn.[78]

As dramatic comedy, *Mostellaria* may engage in dialogue with theatrical ancestors as much as with contemporary folktales or paranormal experiences. Roman theatergoers may well have associated Tranio's story with famous murdered ghosts in drama, such as Clytemnestra in *Oresteia* or Polydorus in *Hecuba*, or Latin adaptations of Greek tragedies that they had seen on stage. Indeed, the most notorious "haunted house" in antiquity is the house of Atreus, whose generations of murdered victims Cassandra describes in vivid, gory detail in Aeschylus' *Agamemnon*.[79]

Pliny's haunted house story, quoted in Appendix 1, offers a representative of the oral and subliterary traditions about the restless dead that Tranio taps into. Pliny asks a friend for advice about the plausibility of ghosts and recounts three eerie anecdotes, including one from his own household. With polished economy, Pliny uses vivid present tense verbs to immerse the reader in the story. The setting is Athens. The ghost (*idolon, monstrum, imago*) of a man improperly buried on the premises appears and terrifies the residents until they sicken and die. For safety, the house remains abandoned until the philosopher Athenodorus, attracted by the cheap price, rents the house. When the ghost appears at night and beckons, Athenodorus follows it to a spot in the courtyard, whereupon it vanishes. Next morning, Athenodorus has local magistrates excavate the spot, where they find bones and chains. The remains receive public burial, and the *Manes* cease to haunt the premises.

Tranio springs his ghost story upon Theopropides immediately upon arrival, which expedites the delineation of the old man's character. The story combines precise, mundane details (such as the unextinguished lamp), with familiar cultural conventions (such as guest–host relationships), with beliefs about ghosts. Murder for gold provides a motive particularly plausible to the businessman Theopropides, and inventing a foreign victim helps explain local ignorance of a crime. Perhaps Theopropides, like Pliny's Athenodorus, acquired the residence at a fantastic bargain. Tranio's servile status might suggest to his master a "spooky" capacity to interface with ghostly apparitions and other paranormal religious agents.[80] Tranio is no Athenodorus, but the philosopher's calm provides a parallel for the slave's fearless claim of "peace with the dead" (514). Actors will have to choose both how smoothly, confidently, and eerily Tranio delivers his narrative amidst interruptions and how credulously Theopropides listens. Exhausted by travels, Theopropides' failure to detect and interrogate inconsistencies can be excused.[81] Plautus faced a choice of dramatic priorities: glorify Tranio or ridicule Theopropides? The more coherent and credible Tranio's ghost story, the less gullible and superstitious Theopropides appears. Or, the less coherent and credible Tranio's ghost story, the more gullible and superstitious Theopropides appears. Since Tranio's character has been established earlier, Plautus stultifies Theopropides, even at the risk of making Tranio seem an unpolished raconteur of ghost tales.

Theopropides ("Son of the Prophet," hence a hereditary trait) becomes a specimen of the Superstitious Man, one of thirty personality types sketched by Aristotle's philosophical successor Theophrastus (371–287 BCE). Theophrastus' cursory *Characters* defines a trait in a single sentence and then gives humorous examples of behaviors by unsavory or ridiculous men who personify that trait, such as the Boastful, Arrogant, or Tactless Man. *Characters* is not a profound work of psychology or ethics. But its comic and often dramatic caricature sketches may have inspired Menander, and its headings do appear as titles for some comedies by Menander, Philemon, and others. Theophrastus defines superstition (*deisidaimonia*) as "cowardice towards the *daimonion*" (the divine, supernatural, or spiritual), and the Superstitious Man is marked by obsessive, irrationally credulous behaviors concerning the supernatural and religious impurity. For example, encountering a snake, weasel, owl, or madman provokes the Superstitious Man to purification rituals. He continually purifies his house and avoids contaminating contacts with birth and death. Theophrastus constructs his characters less from literary tropes than from exaggerations or concatenations of observed habits of real Athenians in their daily lives.[82]

Rome had its share of superstitious people. While it may be rash to assert that one culture is more superstitious than another, Greek Polybius found the Romans quite superstitious. He claims that religious attitudes, especially superstition, made the Roman state superior to the Carthaginian: "it seems to me that this holds Roman society together, I mean superstition [*deisidaimonia*], for in so much pageantry [*ektragōideō*] and to such a great extent is it introduced into their private lives and the commonwealth that nothing could exceed it" (6.56.7–8; note the blurring of public and private spheres). Elitist Polybius asserts that "the multitudes need to be constrained by invisible terrors and suchlike pageantry [*tragōidia*]" (6.56.11). His choice to stress *tragōidia* is remarkable, for the paratheatrical term insightfully yokes the scenic, performative elements that compel a spectator's attention in rituals that we would distinguish as either religious or theatrical. Polybius' eyewitness observations on pageantry, Roman funerals, and superstition jibe with a modern assessment that the "Romans were strikingly preoccupied with, and careful in, their dealings with spirits and shadows," which in turn "would seem to make their nonchalance about the appearance of dead ancestors during the [funeral procession] strikingly odd."[83]

"Nonchalance" may overstate the case, but Romans did perform their daily routines in the presence of deceased noble ancestors, beneath an otherworldly atavistic surveillance. As noted at the start of this section, parts of a noble Roman's house served as a stage for daily performance of social rituals. We know from the passages of Polybius and others that every aristocratic Roman household kept the masks of ancestors in shrines or cupboards in the atrium, the most public part of the house that bustled with daily activities. The cupboards were generally kept closed, so that the masks were not visible, but their presence was known and felt. Every client entering a noble's atrium would know of their presence. Every noble patron would feel the burden of their gaze calling him to accountability and emulation. As Pliny the Younger remarked, the *imagines* seem silently to urge young men to praiseworthy behavior (5.17.6).[84] Our modern homes often have portraits or photographs of ancestors; and given that the Romans usually kept the shrines holding the *imagines* shut, one could argue that we live under a direct ancestral gaze more than they did. Yet whereas our portraits are two-dimensional and static, the three-dimensional Roman *imagines* regularly came back to life at funerals, embodied by actors impersonating the dead.

3

Staging *Mostellaria*

Mostellaria is as fun to see as to perform. While no explication can adequately convey the play's zest on stage, this chapter explores some of the staging presuppositions and opportunities encoded within the script. *Mostellaria*'s minimalist set invites the collaboration of an audience's architectural imagination; its physical comedy catches the eye; its metatheater teases the mind; its ambitious metrical–musical scheme pleases the ear.

The Roman *Scaena*

Different physical settings generate different opportunities and challenges, which in turn generate different sets of conventions for playwrights, actors, and audiences. To the extent that staging follows from architecture, Greek theater is more formal, Roman more improvised and gritty. Rome had no permanent stage dedicated to drama until Pompey's theater in 55 BCE; prior to that, Romans enjoyed "theater without theaters." Plautus wrote for ephemeral theatrical spaces shoehorned into Rome's urban center, with temporary wooden stages amid bustling, irregularly shaped areas that might accommodate a couple of thousand spectators.[1] The physical settings for Roman drama were thus quite different from those of their Greek models, which were produced for the grand permanent stone theaters that we find in hillsides throughout the Hellenistic world, with their excellent acoustics and geometric regularity of stage, orchestra, and semicircular seating to accommodate many thousands.

At least three locations served as recurrent **venues** for plays in republican Rome: the Roman Forum (for the *ludi Romani* and *ludi Plebeii*, as well as for funeral *ludi*); the plaza before the Temple of Magna Mater (for the *ludi Megalenses*); the Circus Flaminius (for the *ludi Apollinares*).[2] The previous chapter suggested how a staging in the Roman Forum would add special resonance to several scenes of *Mostellaria*. Nevertheless, except for a passage in *Curculio*, Plautine scripts do not depend upon site-specific staging. This flexibility made the plays portable to different venues amid the plazas and streets of Rome, or any other town. If some features of *Mostellaria* resemble street theater, we should recall that Roman spectators may have stood on paved streets or sat on temple steps in the very same locations where they witnessed paratheatrical events in their daily routines. Several plays of Plautus feature a prologue speaker demanding silence because the stage had no curtain whose opening would signal the start of a performance. With no prologue, Grumio's yelling (1–5) serves both as a cue calling Tranio onto the stage and as a call for silence heralding the start of the play.

Terminology implies that Greek theater space was audience-centered, Roman theater was actor-centered. The essential feature of a Greek theater was the permanent *theatron* (literally "watching place") adopting the spectators' perspective. The sightlines of the Greeks' semicircular seating fostered a communal experience among citizens watching each other as much as the actors and chorus in their midst. In contrast, Romans identified the locus of their dramatic performances as the **scaena**, the portable stage and onstage spectacle actors generated in front of spectators.[3] Actors occupied the *scaena* (also called the *proscaenium*) and spectators the **cavea**, cheek by jowl because there was no intervening orchestra. Plautus himself uses *theatrum* only once; his preferred term for the physical theater is *cavea*, a "coop" or "cage." *Cavea*'s metaphor from animal husbandry conveys a sense of a noisy, smelly, and cramped enclosure from the perspective of performers on the stage, themselves called a *grex* (herd). The audience is a part of the menagerie but not the essential feature. The pecking order of social stratification entered the theater with the *ludi Romani* of 194 BCE when some seating was reserved for senators (Livy, 34.54.6). While stone temple steps would serve for seating at the *ludi Megalenses*, a location in the Forum would require temporary wooden bleachers, presumably in tiers and frontally facing the *scaena*. The visibility of the Roman cityscape throughout a show maintained a sense of depth around the *scaena* and enhanced a variety of metatheatrical effects.[4]

The Plautine wooden **stage** was a low platform, perhaps a half meter high, perhaps with ramps rather than steps for the entry wings. The width and depth are uncertain and possibly varied based on venue, but a reasonable conjecture for scale would be 9 to 12 meters wide and 3 meters deep in front of the façade.[5] Such dimensions lead to staging that exuberantly flouts naturalism. *Mostellaria* offers typical examples of characters failing to see, hear, or recognize someone only a few meters away, such as with the Moneylender in Scene 5b or Phaniscus and Pinacium in Scene 9a. Slaves supposedly running to announce urgent news take forever to traverse a few meters, like Tranio in Scene 4b. Eavesdropping and asides abound, and Scene 3a with Philolaches and Philematium is the longest eavesdropping scene in Plautus. The lack of spatial realism creates comedy from absurdity and promotes some of Plautus' most distinctive effects in monologue and metatheater. His *scaena* was not a thrust stage, with actors performing amidst spectators on three or even four sides, such as found in early modern English theaters. Its frontal orientation may suggest some similarities to a modern proscenium stage, but Plautine characters regularly address the audience to forbid any modernistic illusion of the "fourth wall."

While the venues may have been diverse, the **set** was uniform: a façade on a street with three doorways, whether all were used in the current play or not.[6] *Mostellaria* gives us the two citizen houses of Theopropides (the play's primary focus) and Simo (the adjacent door, 663). Most likely the unused third doorway has the altar in front of it. By convention, one wing leads to the city and the other to the country and/or harbor. Characters usually announce their destination and origins, so there is no need to propose that in every production the urban center is always to the spectators' right and the country or harbor to their left. A playable organization for the onstage façade and offstage wings of *Mostellaria* would be:

[farm/port] temple – Theopropides' house – Simo's house [urban center]

All the visible action occurs in the street in front of the three doors. By convention, even scenes that should reasonably take place indoors, such as Philematium's grooming and the symposium, explicitly happen in the street.[7] Behind the houses, an alley (*angiportus*) running parallel to the onstage street accounts for any unseen or otherwise inexplicable entrances and exits, as Tranio explains how he circled around via the alley and garden entry to lead the revelers out the house's back door (1043–7).[8]

Much of **Scene 7b** lavishes details on the architecture and decoration of Simo's house, especially the vestibule and walkway (817–18) and the fancy doorposts (818–31). Such passages support the belief that the stage set included vestibules, with two columns per doorway and small porch roofs, or one continuous roof across them. Those columns provide convenient posts for characters to eavesdrop and make asides to the audience. For laughs, not all the described features need be or even should be visible, especially Simo's home decor.[9] The "fresco" of a crow mocking two vultures (832–9) may be a pigment of Tranio's imagination with the metapoetic significance discussed above (p. 16) rather than an actual painted set. Actors' gestures could animate for us a make-believe mosaic *cave canem* into a real guard dog at lines 850–6. Equally, audible barks and snarls offstage or a stuffed dog could prompt Tranio's shushing. Sets can encode memories of previous productions, and possibly Simo's doorposts were distinctive enough to trigger joking allusions to their use in a previous play, such as a palace in a tragedy.[10]

Houses figure as a central feature of *Mostellaria*'s plot and theme. A minimalist set invites maximal imagination from an audience, effectively making us **architects**. One of Plautus' metaphors for the clever slave whose fictions frame a gullible character is the *architectus doli*, the "architect of deceit."[11] He becomes a poet (literally a "maker"), an internal playwright constructing a world of trickery or play-within-a-play. It is tempting to extend the metaphor of architectural cunning beyond Plautine comedy to include both versatile Odysseus and the theatrical architect Vitruvius.[12] *Mostellaria* does not dwell upon the metaphor of *architectus doli*. The only allusion to it is Tranio's veiled self-congratulatory reference to "some architect" who praised Simo's house to Theopropides (760–1). But while Tranio may be the play's only *architectus doli*, Plautus invites us to be the architects in constructing several houses in our imagination, including Tranio's cluttered kitchen, Philolaches' allegorical house, the party den inside, Tranio's haunted house, Theopropides' fantasy renovations, and Simo's house with grand *gynaeceum*, *balineum*, and portico. The publicly visible construction and dismantling of the *scaena* and the façades could reinforce the play's allusions to buildings and remodeling.[13]

Finally, *Mostellaria* has an **altar** to an unidentified deity visible throughout the show, most likely in front of the unidentified third doorway on the side leading to the country and the port. Grumio probably uttered his prayer there upon exiting to the country (77–81), just as Theopropides offers brief thanks to Neptune upon his entry from the port (431–7). His exclamation need not identify the altar as exclusively Neptune's. The altar can generate mild suspense: will it feature in the action as a locus of sacrifice or asylum? Is it a remnant (or precursor) of another drama mounted on the same stage? If an altar by a doorway denotes a temple rather than a domestic shrine,[14] as seems likely for this play, will the temple ever open for someone's entry or exit? We may recall Chekhov's principle that you must not put a gun on the stage if you are not going to fire it. No character exploits the altar until the finale (**Scene 11**), when Tranio activates its latent potential by taking refuge atop it (1094). With ample opportunity for unscripted shenanigans in gesture, pose, and other signs of disrespect, Tranio taunts Theopropides. Tranio literally transforms himself into a *bōmolochos*, the Greek term for a comic buffoon or mocker, named after a species of bird called the "altar-lurker."[15] Wordplay becomes birdplay as Tranio suggests Theopropides boil rather than roast him

(1114–15). Theopropides, being a superstitious man, would never violate the sanctity of the altar by dragging him off. Since altars served as the locus of animal sacrifice (a barbeque, where sacrificial meat would be distributed for eating), the strategy to dislodge Tranio with fire and smoke proves consistent with the landscape of Theopropides' piety.

The slave sitting on the altar appears to have been a popular comic set piece, for we have many statuettes reproducing the image. Especially relevant to *Mostellaria* are the incense burners such as the one reproduced on this companion's cover.[16] The burning incense is placed inside the altar, and the smoke billows from the figure's mouth. Rather than being crazy kitsch, this artifact likely represents a familiar scenario in Roman New Comedy. Theopropides' threat to smoke Tranio on the altar is not idiosyncratic; it is literally iconic. These incense burners suggest a callous wit or sadistic sense of humor among the Roman theatergoers who would choose this trope of comic violence to perfume their homes.[17]

The altar gives Tranio inviolable asylum but not in any explicitly religious fashion. No priest or priestess emerges from the temple to offer him protection, such as in Plautus' *Rudens*. Theopropides' plan to roast or smoke Tranio on the altar gives the play renewed urgency and promises a new twist in the plot. Viewed in terms of theatrical genres, the altar transforms the finale into a comic spoof of suppliant tragedy. Since Tranio cannot escape or even procrastinate punishment through his own agency, only outside intervention can save him. And pat he comes: now sobered up, Callidamates serves as a secular *deus ex machina* (one might say a *deus ex crapula*, "God out of a Hangover"). His intervention saves Tranio and provides the play with a happy ending. If the stagecraft of Plautine slaves occupying the altar spoofed familiar suppliant tragedies, then perhaps *Mostellaria*'s premiere shared a set with a tragedy wherein a divinity had rescued the likes of Iphigenia at the altar. Given that early Roman dramatists adapted and cribbed from Greek tragedians, especially Euripides, we could compare Callidamates with Herakles in Euripides' play of death and ghostly resurrection, *Alcestis*. Herakles enters drunk and disrupts his host's household; he returns sober as a heroic *deus ex machina* to restore a happy ending.[18]

Masks, Characterization, and Actors

One striking feature of Roman New Comedy is its limited number of stock character types: the young man in love; the *meretrix*; the braggart soldier; the pimp; the clever slave; and a few others. The feature appears to blend inheritances from two performance traditions with a typology of masks, Greek New Comedy and Atellan Farce. Menander and Terence, whose characterizations seem more faithful than Plautus' to Greek models, deploy a familiar limited group of stock characters, often with the same names recycled even when they reveal some degree of depth and individuality. Atellan Farce, the preliterary comic pieces from the neighboring Oscans, has an even more limited cast of male characters: Maccus the clown, Pappus the foolish old man, Bucco the braggart, and Dossennus the trickster and/or glutton. For any speculation on the ways in which Plautine characterization blends the two traditions, we are most unfortunate in not knowing to what degree his masks replicated Greek antecedents, or incorporated Atellan elements, or even had features unique to a special character in a particular play. Paintings, mosaics, terracottas, and other artifacts suggest that masks in the *palliata* exaggerated facial features rather than aspired to naturalism.

Character in Roman New Comedy derives from the persona of the mask first, the words of the script second.[19] While readers will appraise a character by examining words in the script, spectators in the theater will form their initial appraisal through visual more than audible signals. A mask instantly communicates the sex and age of a character, and its conjunction with costume, props, and movement establishes social status and occupation. For example, dark hair marks a male character as a young man (an *adulescens* rather than a white-haired old man, a *senex*), and military garb distinguishes a soldier. Although Plautus gives his creations funny, individualized names appropriate to their character, generally "characters are differentiated rather than individualized."[20] Masks telegraph coded expectations of behavior for stock character types. Plautine characters usually conform to those expectations, giving them some affinity with the character types sketched by Theophrastus.[21]

The degree to which Plautus individualizes his creations by fulfilling or foiling expectations within the structure of a given plot is debatable. Some characters clearly deviate little from stereotypical behaviors: Misargyrides is a simplistic moneylender; Theopropides conforms to conventions of a superstitious, gullible, and angry old man. But the characterizations of the partygoers before and after Scene 4 reveal some complexity. Philematium expresses laudable inclinations appropriate to a devoted Roman wife in Scene 3a. She is an ex-*meretrix*, for which there is no specific mask and typology, and Plautus may explore that absence of differentiation via her Roman sentiments. Philolaches, indirectly introduced as prodigal in the opening scene, strikes a contemplative mode in his opening lines (84–7). His long *canticum* in Scene 2 mixes the wish that his father were dead with a remorse that justifies both his contrition and his shame to seek pardon in person at the play's conclusion. Action corroborates Philolaches' allegory that Love can erode one's moral foundations, for he and Philematium seem to behave better when separated, but socializing with peers weakens their better instincts. Callidamates appears as a dissolute *adulescens* with a memorably inebriated entry. He cannot stand, slurs his words, falls asleep, and vows to kill Philolaches' father. This same character returns in the finale as a persuasive orator to mediate between father and son. For these youths, the requirements of a particular scene call forth different facets of character conveyed by the mask.[22]

Human talents animated the masks, and the scripts do provide opportunities for actors to create memorable individuals in performance. While the typology of masks reinforced a coherence and consistency in characterization throughout the Plautine corpus such that most clever slaves or gullible old men resembled each other, we can only wonder to what degree available talent also shaped characterization. We recognize, for example, that Shakespeare's clowns post-1600 are more witty and less rambunctious because Robert Armin replaced Will Kemp. Chrysalus' joke that he loves Plautus' *Epidicus* except when Pellio stages it (*Bacchides*, 213–15) critiques the human talent in a production. Studies of Plautine chronology propose that his later plays are more metrically complex than the earlier as he increased his virtuosity. Perhaps. But equally, having a world-class singer, dancer, or *tibia*-player in the troupe might have encouraged him to expand a role's singing or dancing. Philolaches' *canticum* in Scene 2 is long and even tedious to read, but it may have been a highlight of the performance. Conversely, the absence of such vocal talent might necessitate a simpler play metrically and musically.

A stock of masks enabled **role-doubling**, helping a small cast of male actors play multiple roles. Greek tragedy, as a rule of competition, used only three speaking actors. Scant evidence suggests that rule also held true for Greek New Comedy. Although a few scripts of Plautus can be performed by three speaking actors, Roman New Comedy clearly exploded that rule, as evidenced by its many scenes with more than three speakers.[23] The chief benefit is to enliven the action with a busier stage. Plautus enhances *Mostellaria*'s most boisterous scene (4a, the drinking party) with four speaking—better said, singing—actors. The timing of the scene is surprising, for in three other plays Plautus saves symposiastic scenes to create a grand finale. Tranio's subsequent entry requires five speaking actors onstage concurrently, as well as mute slave attendants. It is unlikely that every speaking part was played by a different actor. Since the economic motive of fewer mouths to feed would encourage a troupe and playwright to strive for the minimum number of speaking actors, devoting one actor solely to play Grumio for *Mostellaria*'s first eighty-three lines would be a waste of resources. We have no evidence that multiple actors shared a single role, though masks would facilitate that possibility, and it is best to assume that they did not.

Appendix 2 gives a plausible doubling chart. For the actors playing Philematium, Delphium, and Callidamates, the assignment of later roles among Simo, Phaniscus, and Pinacium is entirely flexible and can reinforce thematic commonalities. The same actor can play Delphium and Phaniscus as the couch-mates and escorts of Callidamates, but doubling Philematium with Phaniscus reinforces a theme of loyalty. Doubling Callidamates and Simo boosts similarities in their rakish behavior, cretic meters (and associated dance steps?), and intermediary positions between Philolaches and Theopropides. Productions will discover their own benefits in a particular doubling.

It would be wrong to view the economy of actors as a bothersome restriction rather than a tool for conveying meaning. Greek tragedy indicates how dramatists could use an audience's awareness of thematic doubling to positive advantage. For example, having the same actor play both Agamemnon and his son Orestes in *Oresteia* incarnates the themes of revenge and inherited guilt.[24] Role-doubling becomes not an exigency of performance but a desirable compositional technique. We noted above that while Menander seems to have explored relationships between fathers and sons through their direct dialogues, Plautus tends to forgo such interactions by casting the same actor to play both father and son. What need of staging a rapprochement when father is so like son that they inhabit the same actor's body?

Casting the same actor as father and son has profound implications, especially in the closing scene of *Mostellaria*, where Plautus appears to exploit an audience's awareness of role-doubling for thematic and comic affects. Sphaerio's cameo gives an actor ample time to change from Philolaches (final exit into house at 406) into Theopropides (first entry from port at 431). Sphaerio tips the audience to the role-change: "[Philolaches] most urgently ordered me to beg you to scare away his father by any means, so that he won't go inside *ad se*" (into his presence/ to himself, 421–2). With one actor playing both characters, the superfluous *ad se* creates a metatheatrical joke. At the finale (**Scene 11b**), Callidamates excuses Philolaches' absence: "he says that he is afraid to come into his father's sight. Now from our party crew I alone have been assigned as mediator to broker a peace from his father." (1123–7).[25] Fear excuses the casting that precludes a scene of reconciliation. Philolaches cannot show Theopropides contrition, and the father cannot forgive his son directly. The play's focus remains on Theopropides' anger at Tranio's trickery as Callidamates pleads for the slave's pardon, and *Mostellaria* concludes with a promise of continued hijinks from Tranio (or Plautus?). Thematically, our satisfaction comes not at witnessing one family's reunion but at the genre's promise of renewing similar performances tomorrow (1178–9). Callidamates' report that Philolaches "is ashamed to come into your presence because he did what he knows you know" (1154–5) is poignant. When the same actor plays both father and son, the actor's body "knows" who he "did." Theopropides dismisses Philolaches' peccadillos by exclaiming, "with me present, let him make love, drink, do what he pleases" (1164). Theopropides is not a dirty old voyeur; the joke is that "me" and "him" are distinct characters but a singular actor's body. "Theopropides" is necessarily present every time "Philolaches" makes love and drinks. In retrospect, Theopropides' exclamation that his son "acts like his father" (*patrissat*, 639) proves true at ideological, thespian, and corporeal levels.

Additional **mute** performers offer an obvious way to enlarge the spectacle, establish tone, and move larger props expeditiously. Possibly they performed without masks, which safely permits more vigorous slapstick on a stage than is possible with the head's somewhat limited mobility and restricted peripheral vision that results from wearing a mask. *Mostellaria* attests to the presence of mutes in several scenes, most notably the party in **Scene 4**. After Scapha has left the stage, Philematium invites Philolaches to recline for a drink, commands a slave to provide water for washing hands, and commands someone—perhaps a different slave—to set a small table for them (308). The script proves that more than one attendant is present when Philolaches uses a plural imperative for them to remove the drunken Callidamates (385). How many attendants are on the stage we cannot know, but additional hands would help ensure either rapid or chaotically clumsy and noisy removal of such party paraphernalia as the two couches (309 and 327), small table and wash basin (308), and wine jar (347). The plural imperative at line 385 gives textual support for seven as the bare minimum number of performers for *Mostellaria*: five speaking actors, plus two attendants.[26]

In **Scene 5a**, Theopropides arrives with two slave attendants (467). Slaves as porters for travelers are common in New Comedy, and their presence invites us to imagine what sort of luggage they carried. Misargyrides' confidence that Theopropides can pay off the loan suggests that they carry ample and spiffy luggage. Their presence provides opportunities for comic business, such as touching the ground at Tranio's command (46–9). They provide Theopropides with scene partners to address so that he does not think aloud or exclaim to the audience and thereby gain any rapport with us (444). As an internal audience, the porters' postures and gestures can amplify the terror at Tranio's ghost story, and their hasty retreat with the luggage offers opportunities for pratfalls and other stooge-like slapstick.

Simo is accompanied onstage by at least one slave attendant (843), though he clearly owns many (1087–8). When Theopropides asks for slaves and straps to capture Tranio, Simo readily agrees (1038–9), but the script does not make clear if they are visible in the final scene. Theopropides orders them to stand inside the doorway to ambush Tranio when he calls them (1064–5), but he never does call, and his threat to have brushwood brought immediately for smoking Tranio (1114) is never actually given.

Costumes and Props

The genre of Roman New Comedy is defined by the costume: *palliata*. The plays are Greek-inspired comedies in Greek dress, as opposed to the *togata*, Italian comedy in the Roman toga. Free male characters wore a *pallium* (wool cloak) over a tunic, male slaves sometimes simply the tunic. Similarly, female characters wore a *palla* over a tunic. In

Mostellaria, we have no indication that costume marked Misargyrides as a moneylender, so he must proclaim his profession in his entry speech (532–5). Possibly Grumio wore goatskin to mark him as a stinky farmer. If so, the text may encode a joke when Tranio calls him a goat (40) and a mixture of something foul (41).[27] Although ancient symposiasts wore garlands, we see no textual evidence that any of the revelers wore them, and Philolaches impatiently resists the suggestion of applying scented oils.

Female clothing becomes a focal point in **Scene 3a** when Philematium emerges fresh from her bath to put on a dress and sandals. We do not know if the male actor already wears a tunic or a towel conceals his body, perhaps held up by Scapha at the appropriate moments. If a towel, then Philolaches calling Philematium the *Venus venusta* (lovely Venus, 162) could suggest a pose recalling such famous statues as Praxiteles' Venus of Cnidus.[28] As Philematium worries about her choice of dress, Scapha advises her to adorn herself with good morals because lovers love not the dress but its stuffing (168–9). The comment not only introduces the subject of Philematium's loyalties to her liberator discussed in Chapter 2 but also poses a metatheatrical puzzle. Does Scapha critique the tastes only of lovers pursuing their girlfriends, as Philolaches understands it? Or of all males regarding the women they see daily? Or of the male spectators' reception of male actors playing female roles in stage costume?[29] Their discussion touches upon women's clothing and jewelry, possibly with reference to contemporary debates on ostentatious female luxury. Undoubtably members of Plautus' audience, especially women, will have connected the comments about gold jewelry and purple clothing in lines 282–92 with personal experiences with restrictive sumptuary legislation.[30] Something in Scapha's pronouncement on beauty, ornamentation, and morality provokes Philolaches to cease eavesdropping and address them (292–4).

Props in Plautus obtain maximal impact by being minimal in number. Philematium's mirror in Scene 3 not only enables bits of physical comedy but also invites speculation on self-fashioning. Ancient mirrors were of bronze or silver rather than glass, incapable of producing the photographic reflections to which we are accustomed. To what extent do the events on stage reflect or distort a woman's daily performances of social roles in the "real" world? The drinking party requires couches, tables, and cups. How much canoodling could occur on the couches without impeding a masked actor's singing? Actual liquid onstage poses hazards, but empty metal or wooden cups more easily generate or enhance comic soundscapes with their banging, clanging, dropping, and rolling (to say nothing of serendipitous comic opportunities, such as a cup rolling offstage or being left behind). The house key given to Tranio at line 419, emphasized by Sphaerio's cameo, becomes an emblem that this clever slave is trapped and alone with no retreat into the locked house. Does slave Tranio wear a large and visible stage key on a chain around his neck? The double-locked door assimilates him to a modern magician in straight jacket, padlocks, and imminent danger. But unlike a Houdini behind a curtain, Tranio performs his escape through deceptive language before our ears and eyes.

Embedded Stage Directions

Physical components of acting are culturally specific to time, place, and genre. We know nothing of how Roman comic actors learned their parts and rehearsed the concomitant physical elements such as gesture, movement, tempo, or spatial relations. That said, the genre's reliance on stock characters with conventional masks and costumes suggests that the actors employed established routines associated with those character types. Old men move slowly with or without a cane; the "running slave" is a set piece; free young men in love walk but swoon at seeing their girlfriends and cower before their fathers. As each character type has a shtick or several, not unlike the *lazzi* in commedia dell'arte, Roman actors did not require the playwright or a director to block out every movement. The script embeds a key word here and there to cue actors to perform a specific action or begin a practiced physical routine. Let me illustrate with two lively scenes.

Mostellaria's very first word is a cue to an actor to begin and an audience to listen up: *exi* (come out!). The opening exchange in **Scene 1** instructs both performers and spectators that controlling the doorway of Theopropides' home will be the central bone of contention in this comedy.[31] Tranio's objective throughout the play is to secure the portal and drive off all who would terminate the revelry. Consequently, his opening speech crams the preposition *ab* (away) and its compounds six times into ten words (7–8). He punctuates those words by beating Grumio, signaled by an embedded stage direction: "Take that [*em*]! That what you wanted?" "Dammit! Why you beating me?" (9–10). Grumio, seeking to draw Philolaches' debauchery outside for censure and end the party, jams his opening speech with the preposition *ex* (out) and its compounds seven times in five lines. Plautus uses the prefixes to cue the actors to perform their lines with pushing and pulling. The script, unfortunately, does not clarify one crucial aspect of staging the play's opening: does Grumio enter from the countryside wing and bang on a closed door or exit the house and call back inside to Tranio with the door open?[32]

The party in **Scene 4a** offers ample opportunity for physical comedy, and a cluster of embedded stage directions choreographs Callidamates' drunken entry. He smacks one of his slave attendants (*em*! 314) and stutters while asking Delphium if he seems "tit-tit-tipsy" (*mamma-madere*, 319). Stammering on the verb *madere* (to be soused) is funny enough, but since *mamma* means "breast," we may suppose that his head is near, if not resting on, her bosom. Delphium's reply ("you've always diddled away the time that way," 320–1) applies equally to drinking and snuggling. As he staggers in the wrong direction, she yanks him back "*this* way" (*huc*, 321), and they embrace (322–3). Again, he fixates on her breasts as if she were the *alma mater* and he the infant *alumnus* (325a). As he is about to collapse, Delphium teases him with double entendres and holds an unidentified "this" in her hand (328). The "this" most plausibly is his phallus, which need not be a visible part of his costume, let alone the grotesquely large equipment found in Old Comedy.[33] Delphium delivers an aside ("he's soused") to Philolaches and Philematium, or perhaps us, and Callidamates repeats the titsy/tipsy joke (331). After she trades her grip on his phallus for his hand (332), they stumble about together (333), and he tries to stagger back homewards until she redirects him "that way" (335–35a).

Plautine scripts can explicitly direct the masked actors' gestures and movements or the spectators' attention with **deictic** (pointing) words such as *hic*, *huc*, and *hinc* (this here, to here, and from here). In a clear example of deictic gesture and movement, Tranio tells the audience "I'll withdraw from the door to here [*huc*]; from here [*hinc*] I'll spy at a distance" (429). *Hic* can also direct the spectators' attention to someone's entry (e.g., 310, 427, 541, 1063), or spotlight an individual already on stage (e.g., 382, 447, 652, 932, 952). *Hic* sometimes marks frame-breaking asides to the audience. At line 571, Tranio overhears and then tops an aside by Misargyrides: "*This* guy's empty-handed." "*This* guy's certainly a soothsayer." (cf. 566, 778, 784, 963). The deictic words direct the spectators' attention towards a character on stage with emphatic gesture even as the speaker's mask points outwards to address the audience.

The script sometimes announces or spotlights **entries** with phrases such as the deictic *ecce* (look!) or the inquisitive phrase "is that my buddy coming?" (e.g., Callidamates' entry at 310). Sometimes those utterances could serve as cues for an unseen actor to begin emerging from offstage left or right, or even from a doorway, similar to the exclamation that a door creaked and someone is coming out. This preview function is inelegant in reading, but in performance it generates expectation in the audience, especially when a metrical change at a new character's entry or first line provides additional payoff. While readers will know a character's identity from the speech prefix, spectators appreciate an introduction to a new character. For example, at the end of his brief exit monologue (76–83), Grumio behaves as a master of ceremonies in identifying Philolaches, thereby putting a figurative spotlight on the young man and eliminating his need to introduce himself before he bursts into song.

Some entry announcements occur after the entering character is already visible to the spectators, but the speaker remains unaware of the new presence. For example, at the start of **Scene 10** Theopropides watches Phaniscus and Pinacium exit via the harbor/country wing just as Simo enters from the Forum wing. The music stops and Theopropides, believing himself all alone, laments to the audience that he has died. Simo, already onstage, overhears him. After Theopropides finally notices him and tells us "look" (997), Simo taunts him that he has just observed a dead man (1000). Eavesdropping, not coincidence, precipitates Simo's taunt and reifies a hierarchy of rapport (on which, see next section).

The choices of modern editors for where to insert stage directions for entries should not be prescriptive. Likewise, the precise moments of **exits** or invisibility are uncertain. Philolaches orders slaves to carry away the drunken Callidamates (by the armpits? by armpits and ankles? a fireman's carry?), and Callidamates threatens to pee on them unless they give him a chamber pot (385–6). The text gives no precise indication of when he disappears through the doorway, but it is fair to suspect that a kind of "*lazzo* of the drunken exit" prolonged his time on stage.

Imperatives obviously embed stage directions, but I would like to underscore that the simple *em*! (take that!) and *cedo* (give me!) encode status relations. *Em* can assert superiority, especially while punctuating a slap or beating, as Tranio to Grumio (9), Callidamates to a slave (314), or Theopropides to Tranio in reasserting his authority at the play's conclusion (1180). Masters order slaves to give or fetch with *cedo*, as Philematium commands Scapha to give her a mirror and cosmetics (248, 258, 261). But between the sexes, *em* and *cedo* can also establish intimate physical contact, as between Delphium and drunken Callidamates: "Give [*cedo*] me your hand, I don't want you to get hurt." "Take it [*em tene*]." (332–3). Or consider the sexy exchanges of Philematium and Philolaches at lines 297–8: "... my darling." "*Em*! That word's a bargain at twenty minae." "Please, *cedo* ten: I wanna give you that word *bene emptum* (well-bought/well-taken)." His onomatopoetic *em*! (mua!) and her reply of "*cedo* ten ... *bene emptum*" encode actions, almost certainly kisses.[34] Her name, after all, means "little kiss."

Other implied stage directions are opaque or open to multiple interpretations. For example, when Tranio mocks the two old men with his supposed observation of a crow and two vultures (832–40), does the slave-as-seer mimic the poses and gestures of Roman augurs?[35] A strong choice if the play was staged in the Forum where augury occurred. While dancing and singing, does Philolaches mime all his athletic training in discus, javelin, ball, running, weaponry, and riding (151–2)? Or does he vogue a series of poses like those of such famous statues as the Discobolus or Zeus of Artemisium? If actors suit comic action to the word and the word to comic action, then they will discover many other examples during rehearsal that may or may not have been operative in Plautus' Rome. As a colleague quipped with slight exaggeration, to a trained actor performing a script "what word *isn't* an embedded stage direction?"[36]

Monologues, Asides, and Eavesdropping

Plautine theater pervasively engages spectators with three techniques that help dissolve boundaries between a play's internal audience of characters on the *scaena* and its external audience of spectators in the *cavea*: monologues, asides, and eavesdropping. The printed page obscures the prevalence of these features so obvious on the stage. Monologues, asides, and eavesdropping are rhetorical strategies for convincing listeners to adopt a character's or actor's worldview and interpretation of events. They work together to situate figures such as Tranio at a threshold between character and actor, stage world and "real" world, and thereby reify his control of our theatrical experience.

We usually can classify under monologue (one character speaking) the related phenomena of monody (one character singing) and soliloquy (one character speaking while alone on stage). If we include asides, roughly one-sixth of Plautus' plays consist of monologues, and the total rises to roughly a quarter in *Mostellaria*.[37] Plautine theater is not naturalistic and, apart from a few exceptions such as prayers, nearly all Plautine monologues are explicitly or implicitly delivered to the theatergoers. Just as characters use monologue to compete for the confidence of the external audience in the *cavea*, they use dialogue to obtain the confidence of the internal audience on the *scaena*. For example, Philolaches uses monologue to convince us that young men are like houses and he really has a good foundation in Scene 2; Tranio uses dialogue to convince Theopropides that his son has bought a house in Scene 5a.

Asides not explicitly shared between characters on stage are made to us and aim to shape our interpretation of events. On the noisy outdoor stage of Plautus, there are no asides that editors should label with the naturalistic adverb "quietly." By comic convention some characters can address us without it registering in the brains of other characters. That conceit demonstrates how characters making asides enjoy a special, liminal status between the world of the play and the theater audience. Plautus is quite fond of combining asides with eavesdropping. The practice is highly artificial, as eavesdroppers either interject their asides during pauses, or their asides somehow have the power to pause the speech of those overheard.

Analysis of monologues, asides, and eavesdropping in conjunction provides an important barometer for gauging how well some characters succeed and others fail in establishing and maintaining rapport with spectators in what Timothy Moore has dubbed a **hierarchy of rapport**.[38] At the bottom of the hierarchy, some unsympathetic characters deliver no monologues and show no awareness of the theater audience. Above them, some have monologues without explicit recognition of the audience. At the top are characters who can look us in the eye and address us directly, thereby gaining our sympathy and complicity. Asides introduce a level of sophistication to an otherwise simple hierarchy of monologues. Some characters (generally sympathetic) can speak to us without being overheard while others (generally unsympathetic) are subjected to eavesdropping. Eavesdroppers who can make confidential asides to the spectators stand atop the hierarchy of rapport. Their comments frame the spectators' view of the action and can undermine or bolster any sympathy obtained by those who are overheard. Of course, characters can gain or lose rapport throughout the play, and their competition to gain our sympathy need not succeed with everyone. For example: Philolaches ardently appeals for rapport by delivering a monody directly to us in Scene 2 and then assuming the privileged position of making asides while eavesdropping on Philematium and Scapha in Scene 3; nevertheless, any audience member (moralists, farmers, women, soldiers, etc.) may disdain his appeals and dismiss him as dissolute, spoiled, creepy, or cowardly loser.

Since Tranio is the star of the show, I wish to trace his manipulation of monologues, asides, and eavesdropping to reveal the centrality of the hierarchy of rapport to Plautus' dramaturgy. **Scene 1** gives little indication of Tranio's cunning that will secure his triumph. Called out of the kitchen and leaving to buy fish to feed parasitic chums, he may seem little more than a glorified cook. In fact, Grumio has the scene's first and last words alone on stage. Tranio then vanishes for some 270 lines, about a quarter of the play, as Philolaches holds our focus. Suddenly in **Scene 4b**, Tranio bursts onto the stage bearing news that Theopropides has returned from abroad. His entry monologue (348–62) commences building rapport with the audience and hints that he will rise to the challenge even as he expresses his bewilderment. The meter shifts from lyrics to trochees, a signal that the real action now begins with his agency. He breaks through the play's Athenian frame by calling upon slaves and veterans in the Roman *cavea* to undergo crucifixion in his stead (354–60). His monologue enjoys private conference with the theater audience because Philolaches and the other onstage revelers do not hear him (Tranio hails Philolaches first, 363–4). Such is his power that by the end of the play's first arc Philolaches has entrusted his hopes, and we the drama, to Tranio (406).

The second arc commences with Tranio alone on stage for the first time. Changing the meter to calmer unaccompanied iambs, he begins a soliloquy (**Scene 5a**, 409–18). He again presumes a Roman audience, prefacing his claims with reference to the Roman social network of patrons and clients (407–8). He enrolls himself among the clever slaves by promising mischievous deeds with qualifiers typically applied to Plautine tricksters (412–14). The brief interruption of his obedient ally Sphaerio does not sever or diminish his connection with us, for he continues by promising to produce *ludi* for Theopropides (426–30). Having secured intimate rapport with the audience, Tranio can withdraw to eavesdrop on the old man's arrival and treat us to a couple of cheeky asides that belittle his owner (438–9; 442–3).

Theopropides reveals himself as an easy target for Tranio by being gullible, superstitious, and theatrically obtuse. The old man establishes no awareness of the audience, let alone rapport. The start of Tranio's ghost story makes Theopropides' blindness clear:

Tranio

Look around. Is there anyone
who might eavesdrop on our conversation?

Theopropides

It's quite safe.

Tranio

Look around again.

Theopropides

There's nobody.

472–4

The joke equates theatrical blindness with obtuseness, guaranteeing that the old man will be hornswoggled. Tranio directly addressed the Roman audience of eavesdroppers just thirty lines earlier, but Theopropides cannot see that he stands in their midst, even when Tranio doubles down on the gag by telling him to look around again. Now assured that Theopropides has no rapport with an audience that might betray him, Tranio can confidently enlist us as co-conspirators in his plot. Before Tranio can complete his ghost story, the revelers inside the house interrupt in the passage quoted in this companion's Playbill (pp. x–xi). In an aside to us, Tranio frets that they will ruin his fictive play (*fabula*, 510). Theopropides catches the aside only indistinctly because, unable to acknowledge the spectators, he comprehends neither the words nor their audience (519, "who are you talking to?"). Gullible, theatrically naïve, and perhaps even hard of hearing, Theopropides cannot distinguish among voices emanating from behind the façade (noises off), from on the stage, from in the *cavea*.

Tranio, having weathered the initial storm and sent the old man and his entourage running, praises his mischief to us as a mission accomplished ("what a bad bit of business I've done today," 531). But the victory is short lived, as the moneylender enters only one line later (**Scene 5b**). Misargyrides announces his presence and occupation in a four-line monologue, unaware that Tranio overhears him. Tranio tells us that he will confront the moneylender, but in mid-monologue he spots Theopropides returning unexpectedly (536–46). With the moneylender barring one wing exit and Theopropides the other, Tranio is trapped both thematically and choreographically. In a tight spot, his aside to us barely escapes detection by Theopropides (551, "what are you saying to yourself?"). Finding an opening, Tranio reasserts his station atop the hierarchy of rapport first by delivering a short monologue (562–6), then by overhearing the moneylender's attempted asides and capping them with his own confidential asides (566–7, 571).

Tranio can talk to us and eavesdrop, his opponents cannot. Appreciating how Plautus prioritizes the hierarchy of rapport can help avoid the scholarly tendency to view Scene 5b through the anachronistic lens of naturalism. Instead of judging this passage as a defective and awkward attempt to plaster over an act division in the Greek model—as if Plautus lost something in translation because he lacked the ingenuity to avoid having Theopropides and Misargyrides silent for long stretches—we should concentrate on the gains that his choices in staging provide. The sight of Tranio trapped between two blocking figures heightens the urgency above a cleaner sequential confrontation with one opponent then another.[39]

Once Misargyrides exits, Tranio has more space to shore up his intimacy with the audience through an unprecedented stream of asides (655–8, 660, 662–7, 669, 676–7, 678–9 in **Scene 5c**).[40] Those asides make us complicit in his real estate scam. With the fortuitous opening of Simo's door, Tranio confirms his control of the situation in a scene-closing, six-line monologue that concludes with a promise to eavesdrop (684–9). The clever slave again courts his Roman audience through allusions to Roman society, here the senate.

Simo's entry monody marks him as Tranio's tool because he does not perceive the wily slave eavesdropping and making asides (700–1, 711–16). After pleasantries, Tranio springs his trap and shifts the meter to plainspoken iambs to begin a new arc in the action (747). **Scene 6b** is quite short. That the sequence is so short and plain confirms that this challenge is much easier for Tranio to overcome than the double trouble posed by Misargyrides and Theopropides. Smugly self-satisfied, Tranio crowns his brief conversation with Simo by moving to center stage and delivering a monologue in which he compares himself to Alexander the Great and the Sicilian tyrant Agathocles and the old men to mules (775–82). With his control of the stage at its zenith, Tranio can hoodwink Theopropides and Simo quickly and simultaneously rather than seriatim (**Scene 7b**). He can even empower Theopropides to share asides in front of Simo without the latter hearing (810–14, 821–2), as if he were a Hermes able to seal and unseal the eyes and ears of foolish mortals whom he (mis)leads. For our amusement, Tranio mocks the two old men with allegorical jokes about the door posts and the painted crow and, after over 500 lines of intense action, he finally leaves the stage (857).

To remain atop the hierarchy of rapport, one must be present, observing and remarking on all that transpires onstage. Returning to the stage briefly with Theopropides (**Scene 9a**), Tranio fails to observe Phaniscus and Pinacium before making an aside and exiting to meet the revelers (931–2). Tranio's failure to perceive the presence of other onstage actor-characters undermines his station atop the hierarchy of rapport. In his absence, his schemes collapse because Phaniscus and Pinacium reveal the truth to Theopropides. When Tranio returns, he proudly delivers his longest soliloquy, again with allusion to the Roman senate (**Scene 11a**, 1041–63). He thinks that he has triumphed, and we listen with ironic enjoyment at his sudden vulnerability. Given the dullness of his competition, Tranio proves difficult to dislodge from his station atop the hierarchy of rapport. He eavesdrops and makes asides on Theopropides' feeble attempts to act the trickster (1063–73), then decides when and how to confront his master. Adept at stage management, Tranio maneuvers to the safety of the altar to enthrone himself above his outwitted master for the finale.

Metatheater

Plautine comedy is fundamentally metatheatrical rather than naturalistic.[41] Metatheater has become an umbrella term for several phenomena, resulting in imprecision and misunderstandings that bedevil the useful concept. Of the many species within the genus of metatheater, some of which intermingle, I would like to focus on five kinds that have pervasive importance in Plautine comedy.

1. Metatheater denotes plays based upon or responding to preexisting plays or literary works.
2. Metatheatrical moments of non-illusory theater occur when characters puncture the modern convention of an invisible "fourth wall" that separates actors from spectators, such as by directly addressing the audience.
3. More subtly, characters may note their existence as fictions on a stage without necessarily addressing the audience, as when they liken their behaviors to stock characters, or they mark distinctions between an actor's body or mind and a character's mask or persona.
4. Characters who behave as theater practitioners that script, direct, or perform a play-within-the-play create metatheater.
5. Metatheater holds a mirror up to the performative and theatrical nature of social life, as if all the world's a stage whose role-playing drama exposes.

Our analysis has touched upon several of these types already, but it is worth consolidating some of those earlier observations, introducing a few more instances, and then giving an example of how they intermingle.

Regarding the first type, we observed in Chapter 1 how *Mostellaria* mocks Diphilus and Philemon. But without access to those specific Greek New Comic models, it is difficult to assess how Plautine passages may replicate, extol, or spoof those ancestors. Unlike some other Plautine plays, *Mostellaria* contains no passages we can identify as overt parody of a specific tragedy or comedy. At a generic level, Callidamates' entry at the finale may recall a *deus ex machina* from suppliant tragedies (see pp. 58–9). And we may always suspect that some sequences in Plautus reprise his own earlier works rather than Greek models or Roman antecedents.

The previous section examined a hallmark of the second type of metatheater, in which Plautine characters directly address their audience in monologues and asides. Non-illusory addresses to the spectators are often implicit and do not require explicit verbs and pronouns such as "listen up, y'all." The lines from **Scene 5a** quoted above, in which Tranio tells Theopropides to look around for eavesdroppers, merits further consideration here. In naturalistic theater, where the characters have no awareness of the audience, the exchange is unremarkable. In Plautus' non-illusory metatheater, the exchange exploits the fundamental joke that the actor-character Tranio knows that they emphatically are not alone but are overheard by thousands of listeners. *Aucupet* (eavesdrop, 472) literally means "go fowling" or "wait in ambush." Plautus often uses the word for eavesdropping, perhaps for its metatheatrical implication of the *cavea* (bird coop) holding the audience. Does Tranio sweep his arm to the crowd as Theopropides cranes his neck around? Once we recognize Tranio's ability to address us as a complicit audience, we can appreciate how Plautus' script provides that actor with playable choices based on non-illusory metatheater. In **Scene 7b**, while mocking Simo and Theopropides outside the doorposts Tranio quips "Look how snugly they sleep" (829). Theopropides naturalistically applies the comment to the door bolts and is puzzled by the animation of "they sleep." Tranio emends it to "they're shut." If the actor playing Tranio adopts the stronger choice of directly addressing the audience with "they sleep" while indicating the old men, then we share in his stream of metatheatrical wisecracks.[42]

In the third kind of metatheater, characters acknowledge their existence as dramatic fictions. The device is common in Plautus but rarely indicated as overtly as at the opening of *Mercator*, where the young man tells the audience, "I'm not acting like I've seen other guys smitten with love act in comedies" (3–4). We sometimes must read between the lines to uncover the oblique allusions that sufficed for Roman audiences familiar with the genre's actors, characters, and routines. For example, the section on role-doubling noted how both Theopropides and the Callidamates allude to the likelihood that the same actor played father and son. When the action of *Mostellaria* accelerates at the opening of **Scene 4b**, Tranio bursts onto the stage with a monologue announcing that he has seen Theopropides at the harbor. He performs the role of a tragic messenger bearing news that will kill the party. But rather than hasten to tell Philolaches (who is only, after all, a few meters away), the actor-character stops to banter with the audience in a direct appeal for a surrogate Roman soldier to suffer crucifixion (354–61). In a moment revealing his awareness of the comic genre, Tranio muses "But I . . . ain't I a wretch not speeding home at full speed [*curro curriculo*]?" (362). He refuses to play the stock comic routine of the *servus currens*, the running slave, in which the bearer of urgent news takes forever to traverse the stage while addressing the audience in a monologue.[43]

The fourth type of metatheater animates some of Plautus' most famous plays when tricksters frame their deceits as a play-within-a-play. Tricksters both male and female in *Bacchides, Casina, Epidicus, Miles Gloriosus, Persa, Poenulus, Pseudolus,* and others construct a plot, instruct their crafty helpers in the roles they must play, sometimes disguise them in costumes, and in two cases even explicitly liken themselves to playwrights. In a monologue to us, Tranio the impresario promises to stage *ludi* for the living Theopropides, as if for his funeral (427). His first show must be solo and improvised because his helpers are in such varied states of inebriation that he cannot script roles for them. In fact, their untimely knocking on the door almost ruins his play-within-a-play (*fabula*, 510) about the ghost at the outset, and Theopropides quickly discovers the fabrication from the house's previous owner. Tranio's second show, the fiction that Philolaches bought a house, poses an entirely different challenge.[44] Again he is solo, doing the greatest immortal deeds equal to those of Alexander the Great but without troops or a troupe (775–7). As theatrical director, he must coax the desired performances out of two unwitting actors, Theopropides and Simo. Since Tranio cannot reveal his play-within-a-play to them, he gives different false motivations and objectives to each one. He instructs Simo on how to treat Theopropides as an emulous home renovator. He coaches Theopropides on how to treat Simo as a foolish and remorseful seller, especially in lines 810–14 with his directorial tips on facial expression, gestures, and "seeming."

As for the fifth type, Chapter 2 placed *Mostellaria* within its Roman cultural context of such paratheatrical events as aristocratic funeral pageants, the feasts associated with the *ludi scaenici*, and the bustle of the Roman Forum. We may add here that Philolaches' monody (**Scene 2**), with its non-illusory direct addresses to his audience (96, 100), appropriates the diction and structures of oratory. Apparently trained in literature, law, and legislation like a Roman aristocrat (126), he pleads a rational case to his audience as if they were an assembly of jurors or voters. On normal workdays, many of them were. Translation obscures some of the legal and oratorical connotations of his vocabulary, such as *res* (case: 92, 99, 100), *argumenta* (arguments, proofs: 85, 92, 99, 118), and *arbitror* (testify, judge: 89, 91, 119). Philolaches' rhetorical posture would have gained extra resonance if the staging area were in the Forum at or near the *comitium*, the central locus for political oratory. His song mirrors serious civic activities and reveals that they, too, are just acts. As Cicero the orator can imitate comic figures in his *pro Caelio*, so Plautine comic figures can imitate orators.[45] The interpenetration began long before Cicero, such that we must wonder whether oratory or theater is the "meta" borrowing from the other.

These five metatheatrical techniques intermingle, such that analysis isolating and prioritizing a single species risks underappreciating the total ecosystem. Those who prefer the modern theatrical convention of naturalism may find Philematium's toilette in **Scene 3** tediously long and ridiculous for being set in the street. Possibly so. But the scene's success in performance largely derives from its accumulation of metatheatrical elements. Scapha's aphorism that lovers do not love a dress but rather its stuffing (168–9; see p. 65) stands as commentary not only on the objectification of women in Roman comedy and society but also on the performative nature of gender in theater and life. The prop of the mirror suggests that Philematium, or the actor behind the woman's mask, holds a mirror up to society. Male actors performing in drag reveal the putative secrets of sexual attractiveness in life and art. As noted below, the meter in Scene 3a is commonly featured in scenes with *meretrices* and lovers, an auditory marker of a comic set piece. With some consciousness that they are acting like stock New Comic characters, Scapha plays the role of the cynical bawd, Philematium the loyal *meretrix*, and Philolaches the dopey young lover. Philolaches eavesdrops with asides, including an explicit direct aside to the audience (280–1). As young lover, his praises of Philematium and critiques of Scapha become a bit insipid. As theater critic, some of his comments incisively evaluate how successfully the characters (or actors?) perform the stock roles of *meretrix* and bawd. Scapha earns rather uneven reviews: at times charming (170, 171, 252, 260, 271) and worthy of applause (260); at times forgetting a line (184) and inconsistent in characterization (257); at times praised with adjectives usually reserved for the clever slave (270 *callida*, 279 *docta*). When Philolaches finally abandons the role of spectator to greet Philematium, the shtick concludes with self-consciously theatrical vocabulary: "What are you performing [*agis*] here?" "I'm costuming myself [*me exorno*] to please you." "You're adequately costumed [*ornata es*]" (293). Such comments suggest that the scene may contain bits of improvisatory expansion.

Improvisation

Improvisation is an umbrella term covering a range of sequences from fully scripted and rehearsed that only seem improvised (feigned improvisation), through bits mixing rehearsed components and flexible general routines (shtick; cf. *lazzi* in commedia dell'arte), to completely unrehearsed, extemporaneous ad libs. Our term "script" prioritizes the written word, but all the prepared bits of physical performance are also "scripted" through rehearsal. In feigned improvisation, only the character improvises because the actor still follows a script, as when Tranio confides to us in an aside "I don't know what to say now" (676 and 678). Of course, the actor knows his or her next line! In ad libs, the actor truly creates something impromptu off script, sometimes stretching or even breaking what we might consider the limits of character. Every performance will have moments—words, gestures, interruptions, etc.—that are fully improvised. But unless successful ad libs become incorporated into subsequent performances, they vanish from memory. On the other hand, once incorporated into the text, they cease to be ad libs.[46]

Cue lines provide actors with textually stable boundaries. Improvisation both verbal and physical is easier in the middle of monologues prior to a character's final scripted words that provide the cue for a scene partner to speak. For example, Tranio's first soliloquy can be expanded or contracted based on audience response, but whatever his improvised verbal and physical antics, the actor must finish the routine with the movements and words "and I … ain't I a wretch not speeding home?" (362) to provide the cue for Philolaches to speak.

Meter can shape verbal improvisation. All plays of Plautus are in verse, and almost two-thirds of the verses had musical accompaniment. Simply put: to what extent could an actor go off script without confounding the musical accompanist or a scene partner? At one end of the spectrum, the unaccompanied verses in iambs allowed some freedom, just as the English iambic pentameter allows actors dropping, botching, or inserting lines to keep rolling. At the other end, verses in complex and shifting meters (*cantica*) must have required more precision and choreographed rehearsal, and thus allowed little to no room for *ex tempore* elements. In between, the sequences of musically enhanced trochees and iambs exhibit somewhat predictable metrical regularity, especially at line ends, which suggests a rhythm sufficiently repetitious to accommodate improvisation. Improvised words and phrases would fit into metrically framed verses or chunks of a verse. We might compare how Homeric poets fit flexible and sometimes formulaic chunks into the dactylic hexameter rather than recited verbatim an inflexible, memorized text.[47]

Sequences that do not advance the plot suggest the insertion or expansion of flexible, transferable *lazzi* by either Plautus or later companies. For example, the sequence 575b-610 in **Scene 5b**, in which Misargyrides duns Philolaches and Tranio tries to silence him, appears to be a stock loan-shark routine with no specific details tied to *Mostellaria*. Remove it and the dialogue flows smoothly from line 575 into 611: "Where's Philolaches?" "You couldn't have come to me at a more opportune moment." "Why's that?" "C'mere. [. . .] Look, his dad just arrived from abroad . . .". Cutting or abridging the loan shark *lazzo* quickens the pace but sucks the improvisatory lifeblood out of Plautus.[48]

The impromptu nature of Tranio's scheming suggests that *Mostellaria* is constructed from blocks of flexible, improvisational *lazzi* rather than an intricately scripted, fully rehearsed plot. Some of Plautus' most accomplished tricksters form a plan, rehearse their helpers, then oversee execution of that plan. Tranio has no plan and no helpers. *Mostellaria* presents his single-handed, bravado, impromptu solutions to a series of crises and confrontations with other characters: the assault of Grumio; the return of Theopropides; a party in front of the house with someone passed out; a moneylender dunning in Theopropides' presence; his ghost story refuted; Simo meeting Theopropides; Theopropides' discovery of the deceits and ambush. If *Mostellaria* seems like a kaleidoscope of *lazzi*, perhaps Plautus, like Tranio, conjured up a production befitting someone's *ludi funebres*. As Sander Goldberg observes, "[f]uneral games . . . always had a distinctly improvisational element, and not only because they so often came on short notice."[49]

Meter

Aulus Gellius records the supposedly autobiographical epitaphs of Naevius, Plautus, and the tragedian Pacuvius, of which Plautus' reads: "Since Plautus has died, Comedy mourns, the *scaena* is deserted, then Laughter, *Ludus*, and Wit, and *Numeri innumeri* all wept together" (*Attic Nights* 1.24). Though likely apocryphal, the epitaph rightly touts Plautus' stagecraft, ludic spirit, and *numeri innumeri*, "countless meters." Plautus was an acknowledged master of Latin lyric meters, inviting us to consider him as a librettist as much as a dramatist. His plays were musical comedies, whose verses modulated among unaccompanied iambs, trochees and iambs accompanied by the *tibia*, and intricate *cantica* or songs in mixed meters accompanied by the *tibia*. Short of multicolor printing or varied fonts, the effects of these modulations are impossible to countenance on the page. Nevertheless, a brief introduction to Plautine meter can help us appreciate how his virtuosity in versification shapes three areas of his compositions: characterization; tone of a scene; and structure of the action.[50]

The two most common metrical units (or "feet") in Plautus are the iamb and the trochee, with roughly 89 percent of his verses in these basic forms. In Latin, a pure iamb is a metrical unit with two components called "short" (or "light") followed by "long" (or "heavy"), often marked in texts with ˘ ¯. It resembles but is not identical to the English iambic foot of two *syllables*, unstressed then stressed (as in the word "begin").[51] In Latin poetry, as in English or ancient Greek, a sequence of iambs can closely resemble the flow of ordinary speech, and in Roman New Comedy verses in iambic senarii (six iambic units; designated ia^6) were spoken, unaccompanied by music. Plautus uses ia^6 to convey important plot points with clarity, to conform to episodes of lower emotional intensity, and even to mark characters as unsympathetic drudges. Roughly 37 percent of Plautus' verses are in unaccompanied ia^6; about the same percentage is found in *Mostellaria*.

A pure trochee is a metrical unit of two components, long followed by short, often marked as ¯ ˘. It resembles but is not identical to the

English trochaic foot of two syllables, stressed then unstressed (as in the word "study"). By beginning with a long unit, a sequence of trochees often sounds more insistent and less conversational than iambs. Verses in trochaic septenarii (seven trochaic units; designated tr^7) were accompanied by the *tibia*, musically bolstering the trochee's sense of energy, emotional intensity, even staginess. We are uncertain of how actors delivered tr^7. Most likely its rhythm and musical enhancement produced something more patterned than ordinary speech, if not quite song; some varieties of beat poetry, rap, or preaching offer an intriguing range of comparisons.[52] Tr^7 is the most common meter in Plautus (roughly 41 percent; it dips to about 34 percent in *Mostellaria*), a far higher percentage than found in Menander or Terence. That fact alone establishes Plautus' dramatic priority as conscious performativity rather than any species of naturalism.

Roughly another 11 percent of Plautus' longer verses employ other forms of musically enhanced trochees and iambs, such as trochaic octonarii (eight units; tr^8; rare), iambic septenarii (seven units; ia^7; over 6 percent) and iambic octonarii (eight units; ia^8; about 2 percent). Scene 3a of *Mostellaria* is entirely in ia^7. All told, roughly 52 percent of the Plautine corpus consists of musically enhanced trochaic and iambic verses; 42 percent in *Mostellaria.*

Finally, and most remarkably, Plautus composed sequences in lyric meters we call *cantica* (singular: *canticum*). He did so for solo songs (monodies), duets, or ensemble scenes. Plautus was not only a playwright; he was Rome's first great lyric poet. We shall briefly examine a few *cantica* relying on two of his favorite lyric meters, bacchiacs (˘ ¯ ¯) and cretics (¯ ˘ ¯). While some *cantica* in Plautus do rely entirely or mostly upon a single meter, frequently the meter changes from line to line in bewildering complexity. *Cantica* introduce a wide variety of effects for characterization and emotional tone of a scene. Overall, roughly 11 per cent of Plautine verses, but a hefty 20 percent of *Mostellaria*'s, are *cantica.*

Characterization emerges as much from a preferred type of verse as from a mask or diction. Whether characters speak or sing their lines reveals their personality to the actors learning their lines, and thence to an audience. A glance at Appendix 3, which gives rough figures for types of meter by characters in *Mostellaria*, indicates a character's basic disposition. Grumio and Misargyrides—the single-scene killjoys whose presence threatens Tranio's control and the revelry—only speak iambs without musical accompaniment. In strong contrast, the revelers (Philolaches, Philematium, Delphium, Callidamates) and their slave attendants (Scapha, Phaniscus, Pinacium) speak no *ia*^{6} and deliver all their lines with musical accompaniment. Notably, the women speak no *ia*^{6}. Scapha, being older and not participating in the festivities, delivers *ia*^{7} and *tr*^{7} but does not sing in mixed meters like the young. Tranio, Theopropides, and Simo are the only characters inhabiting all three modes. Their metrical variations underscore how Tranio's real estate scheme depends upon their changing mindsets.

Monodies allow uninterrupted self-presentation. Philolaches introduces himself to us directly in a long monody in **Scene 2**. With some tedium, readers can follow his exposition of how a youth resembles a house and his conflict between discipline and indulgence. With pleasure, audiences will feel the exposition and the conflict in the metrical alternation of bacchiacs and cretics, as if a symphonic psychomachia. Bacchiacs tend to feel serious, cretics festive. Based on meter, the *canticum* falls into four parts: the building of the house in bacchiacs and iambs (84–104); its destruction in cretics and trochees (105–17); building of a youth's character in bacchiacs and iambs (118–32); its destruction in cretics and trochees (133–56).[53] The meter suggests turns in choreography not unlike the strophe and antistrophe of a chorus in Greek tragedy: the actor's movements back and forth on stage would provide visual reinforcement to the thematic and auditory swings.[54] However Plautus then or a director now might handle Philolaches' song, there must be significant audible distinction between the alternating sections of resolute bacchiacs and dissolute cretics. Philolaches is prodigal but not inherently bad or a thoroughly lost cause. His song must reveal his good moral foundation, self-awareness, education, and remorse. He may not succeed in gaining our sympathy, but at least he has enough shame to try.

After an extraordinarily long segment of *ia*^{6} in Scene 5, the *canticum* in **Scene 6a** introduces Simo as a merry old man sympathetic to the revelers and willing to keep their secret from Theopropides. As the music starts, Simo begins singing in cretics, a bouncy lyric meter that Plautus often uses for joyful farce. Simo proclaims his happiness with an excellent lunch, then rakishly confides that he is sneaking off to avoid sleeping with his wife. Seeking to build rapport with the audience, he sings to us with direct address (709). Eavesdropping Tranio makes asides to the audience in the same meter (700–01, 711–17), thereby inserting himself (and keeping us) within Simo's emotional realm rather than establishing himself (and us) at a critical distance via any snarky change of rhythm. Finally, Tranio greets Simo in cretics (717), a sly token of friendly conformity, and Simo asks when today's party will begin, perhaps angling for an invitation. We sense that they have had similar friendly exchanges over the past three years.

In exploring interactions between characters, we should observe who takes the lead and who conforms to a metrical change. After joining Simo's cretic *canticum*, Tranio inserts two verses of trochees to lament that their party boat now lacks a favoring wind and is about to be rammed by another ship (737, 740). Metaphorically, the image befits Theopropides' arrival at port. Rhythmically, those two trochaic verses sink the buoyant tone of Simo's cretics and shift the emotional ballast of their conversation away from a *canticum*. Simo accepts Tranio's cue, and verses 741–5 switch to *ia*^{8}, a meter Plautus sometimes uses for tragic parody or to instill a sense of closure.[55] A shared line of *ia*^{7} seals their alliance to keep the secret, after which they switch to clear, plainspoken *ia*^{6}. The party is indeed over, and we hear the festivity winding down in the progression of *ia*^{8} to *ia*^{7} to *ia*^{6}.[56]

Meter can suggest winding down or revving up of pace and emotional intensity. Like the musical score in a film, meter sets and enhances the **tone** for a scene. Transitions such as the one just described are especially significant. Does a character introduce a new meter that is embraced or resisted by another? Does an entry or exit prompt a metrical change? Of what sort?

The end of Philolaches' *canticum* in Scene 2 winds down from cretics to three verses of *tr*⁷ as he laments how defects in his character make him worth "nothing" (154–6). Perhaps he sits down or collapses like his allegorical house. But then, unforeseen, Philematium and Scapha enter in a jolly mood. Philematium sets that tone of **Scene 3a** by beginning their exchange in *ia*⁷ (and presumably entering first, the stronger position). Given the frequent association of *ia*⁷ with *meretrices* in both Plautus and Terence, these accompanied iambs "could be called the meter of love."[57] Philolaches adopts their meter, immersing himself and the audience into their emotional world. He waxes poetic about Venus, Cupid, and Love, linking them to the storm that ruined his house (162–5), but he does not engage the women directly until line 293, assuming a superior position in the hierarchy of rapport through surveillance with eavesdropping and asides. The meter and Philolaches' voyeurism cast Philematium as an object of love even as she and Scapha explore her subjectivity. As discussed in Chapter 2, the women engage in spirited debate over moral duties to her liberator, elevating their exchange above banal expressions of infatuation. Scapha, fearing a beating (247), finally concedes to Philematium. Immediately in the next line, Philematium takes the initiative in changing the meter to *tr*⁷, providing a clear auditory marker to end the debate. She calls for her mirror and jewelry, a visual cue that she wishes to change the topic. Scapha (and Philolaches) follows her mistress to *tr*⁷ and counsels her on the use and abuse of mirrors, cosmetics, perfumes, hairstyles, and dresses until Philolaches interrupts them.

In conjunction with *tibicen*, the character introducing a metrical shift sets the tone. After Tranio successfully ensnares Simo with trickery in *ia*⁶, he boasts to us of his deeds equal to those of Alexander the Great and Agathocles (775). Turning his attention back to Theopropides in **Scene 7a**, at line 783 Tranio initiates a change from unaccompanied *ia*⁶ to a *canticum* of bacchiacs and leads his owner to Simo's doorway. Plautus often uses bacchiacs for exchanges between masters and slaves.

Bacchiacs can also tend to drag, allowing Plautus to establish a tone of seriousness, mock-seriousness, or to "slow other characters down."[58] Tranio tells us that he will approach the old man and then greets him (783–4). Master Theopropides accepts the invitation to bandy bacchiacs, and they sing their verses while strolling to Simo's house. Ideas conform to the meter, as their lines repeatedly emphasize delay, sluggishness, and waiting (787, 789, 794, 795, 803), thereby highlighting tensions between an owner's commands and a slave's obedience. When at last they traverse the stage to Simo's doorway, Tranio shifts the meter to tr^8 (804). Simo greets Theopropides with a metrical change to tr^7 (805) and opens his home to inspection for a new sequence of action.

The drinking party (Scene 4a) and the monody of Phaniscus (Scene 8a) deploy a dizzying variety of meters, truly *numeri innumeri* beyond the scope of this companion.[59] Here especially our discussions are hamstrung. Despite all that we can glean from metrical analysis, the sad fact remains that we have only Plautus' lyrics and metrical schema—the sheet music for his rhythms—but not the tempos or melodies actualized by musicians and actors. That lack places severe limitations on our interpretations. For a very crude analogy that ignores melody and instrumentation, we quickly recognize the 3/4-time signature of a Waltz or the clave of Afro-Cuban genres. Even if we cannot precisely articulate it, those rhythms alone convey certain cultural and emotional connotations. Nevertheless, without tempo or melody we may not know if (e.g.) a samba is upbeat or melancholy. We do not know how the contributions of the *tibicen*'s tunes and the actors' voices fleshed out the rhythmic skeletons Plautus provided. We do not even know if a similar melody accompanied a character or meter as a leitmotif. For example, did the *tibicen* craft a "Callidamates theme" or melodic tag used with both his cretics and trochees? Were snippets from Philolaches' clash of fun-loving cretics and edifying bacchiacs reprised in Simo's postprandial cretic entry and Theopropides' bacchiac promenade to tour Simo's house? Modern directors will have to make a choice.

The five acts and many scenic subdivisions found in most texts and translations of Plautus are modern inventions with no ancient authority.

Unlike Greek New Comedy, Roman New Comedy was performed with continuous action uninterrupted by four choral interludes. A Plautine play's **structure** of events and pace of performance depends to some degree on scenes marked by a major character's entry or exit, and to a greater degree on significant metrical changes. The Synopsis reveals *Mostellaria*'s alternation of ia^6 and verses with musical accompaniment. Since there is no hard rule for labeling scenic divisions, I have marked subdivisions based upon meter, for example in Scene 3 when the meter changes from ia^7 to tr^7 with no entry or exit. In performance we would hear the change but not consider it a new scene, hence my designations "3a" and "3b." In watching a play on the stage without intermissions or choral interludes, the experience of scenes will differ greatly from what one reads on the page.

In grouping units of action, Toph Marshall has proposed that we observe a play's progress through metrically marked "arcs."[60] Plautus generally begins an arc with spoken ia^6 and follows directly with tr^7, but sometimes he inserts a more complex *canticum* before the simpler tr^7. As Timothy Moore puts it, the onset of tr^7 will "send the message 'OK, enough of whatever else we have been doing: now let's get on with the plot.'"[61] Tr^7 also seems to mark the end of an arc or unit of action. Nearly every Plautine play concludes with tr^7, and the two exceptions end in celebratory *cantica*. The progression from ia^6 to tr^7 appears common enough to consider it a pattern that might be anticipated by an audience. Exposition occurs in ia^6, and resultant vigorous action follows in tr^7. Sometimes in between them a lyric *canticum* provides emotional exploration of the exposition or marks a surprising new arrival. The Synopsis shows how *Mostellaria* falls into four arcs, each beginning with ia^6.

If a progression from ia^6 through *canticum* to tr^7 is a norm, it is clearly not an ironclad rule, and the pattern is flexible enough to admit meaningful exceptions.[62] Twice *Mostellaria* shows the expected progression in reverse, with transitions "backwards" from tr^7 to *canticum* (Scenes 3b to 4a, 7b to 8a). In between those retrogressions, the second arc contains the longest continuous stretch of ia^6 in Plautus

(Scene 5). Tranio's ghost story avails him nothing, as immediately he must fend off both Theopropides and the moneylender. Tranio's inability to shift from the unaccompanied meter into dynamic tr^7 audibly reinforces his lack of progress. Since the second arc does not resolve anything, it does not end with tr^7. Grinding its metrical gears, it lurches straight from Simo's *canticum* back into ia^6 as Tranio must now trick Simo (6a-b). I believe that *Mostellaria*'s form replicates content. Tranio does not have an elaborate plan that he can smoothly implement; rather, he improvises, lying to counter the arrivals of Theopropides, Misargyrides, and Simo. The farcical, non-linear plot justifies flouting the normal orderly metrical progression towards resolution in ia^6 – *canticum* – tr^7.

Farce and Low Resolution

Modern half-hour sitcoms give us roughly twenty-two minutes of action, plus commercial interruptions. Early modern audiences of Shakespeare, Jonson, and Heywood would enter the theater expecting approximately two hours' traffic on the stage. Such benchmarks allow spectators to gauge progress towards resolution. But watching a play of Plautus, we often have no idea whether it will be short like *Curculio* or *Epidicus* at roughly 730 lines, or double that length like *Miles Gloriosus* or *Rudens* at roughly 1430 lines. The alternation of spoken ia^6 and accompanied verses provides relative rather than absolute gauges of progress. If we expect a play to end in tr^7, we cannot be certain whether a scene adopting that meter will prove to be the finale or just another delaying complication. The number and length of arcs is unpredictable.[63]

Some critics have complained of *Mostellaria*'s freewheeling plot even as they praise its comic zest. The play's lack of structure frustrates those preferring an Aristotelian dramatic scheme of beginning, middle, and ending. *Mostellaria*'s action sticks in the middle. The plot properly begins with Theopropides' return at line 348, about one-third of the way through the play's 1181 verses. The arbitrary rather than causally necessary ending denies any sense of resolution when Tranio promises more deception tomorrow. As if to preempt any dramatic criticism, Tranio touts the play's lack of forward progress as an improvement upon the tidy teleological aesthetic of Greek New Comedy in the passage quoted in Chapter 1: "If you're a friend to Diphilus or Philemon, tell 'em by what scheme your slave tricked you: you'll 've given 'em the best deceptions [*frustrationes*] for comedies." (1149–51). *Frustrationes* also means "delays," as Misargyrides complains of frustrations at line 589. Through his mouthpiece Tranio, Plautus boasts of crafting the best delays in New Comedy to make space for the farcical deceptions that produce laughter. Tranio engages in seemingly improvisatory shenanigans that can only delay Theopropides' discovery of the truth. Tranio is like an actor improvising comic bits that—to our delight—delay the forward momentum of the plot.[64]

Plautus scripts delays from the beginning, as *Mostellaria* jumps without a prologue into the middle of activity going nowhere. The first arc—roughly 30 percent of the play—dissolves chronological time to present kaleidoscopic farce. Its scenes could be rearranged, abridged, or even omitted with minimal adjustment or loss of comprehension. While the opening four scenes delightfully develop character, a traditional analysis of plot would reveal their lack of progress and interchangeability in sequence: in Scene 1, a dialogue between slaves establishes Philolaches' prodigality; in Scene 2, Philolaches himself sings of his prodigality; in Scene 3, Philolaches eavesdrops upon and speaks with Philematium, the cause of his prodigality; in Scene 4, their party with two friends demonstrates the prodigality. We could posit a sophisticated movement from hearsay to introspection to cause to effect, but clearly the first arc prioritizes sprawling and recurrent fun over tight and linear plot development.[65] Such anti-structure may have been a virtue in Rome's outdoor public venues, with spectators drifting in and out and the play quite possibly reperformed on successive days.[66] *Mostellaria* is not unique in its deployment of false starts, restarts, delays, and lack of progress. *Pseudolus* deploys the same techniques and even celebrates them with metatheatrical comments calling attention to that play's delicate balance between indulging in crowd-pleasing tangents and keeping the plot moving toward resolution.[67]

The promise of more hijinks tomorrow, in fact, precipitates the ending of today's play. Perhaps I have given too much credit to the persuasive powers of Callidamates. When Theopropides agrees to let Tranio go in **Scene 11b**, form indicates that Callidamates' agency is decisive because he shares a line with the old man (1180). But content suggests that Tranio's bargain to endure double punishment tomorrow for today's and tomorrow's mischief (1178–9) proves irresistible to Theopropides the investor, who is willing to exact more profitable revenge in the future. As a metatheatrical epigram, Theopropides delivers the play's final line in direct address to the audience: "spectators, *this* play [*fabula haec*] is finished: applaud!"[68] But his business with Tranio is not resolved, only delayed. His assertion that the only thing finished is today's performance of *this* play doubles as promissory note to the audience that they can return tomorrow for a new play or a repeat performance. But to cash in, you must come back.

Mostellaria's plot is stuck in the middle because it cannot reach the resolutions available to other Plautine plays. It cannot proceed towards a long-awaited union of young lovers because Philolaches already has purchased Philematium's freedom and has enjoyed unlimited access to her. It cannot proceed towards citizen wedding because, as a former *meretrix*, Philematium is unmarriageable. It cannot proceed towards a celebratory banquet today because Scene 4a already staged the party, and Simo (or the actor?) angles for a dinner invitation chez Theopropides tomorrow (1006–7). Theopropides cannot even reconcile with Philolaches because the same actor most likely played both father and son. But rather than lament the absence of such tidy resolutions, we do better to celebrate the triumph of non-teleological farce over finality. If a comedy ends with reconciliations and marriage, that's nice, but that's all, folks. Tranio's play is never finished. In him, the inextinguishable spirit of the trickster stands ever ready for reincarnation tomorrow.

4

Afterlife and Ghost Lights

This chapter spotlights selected significant events in *Mostellaria*'s transmission from Rome to today. After indicating how the play's textual history shaped the current script, it explores three partial reincarnations of *Mostellaria* in early modern English plays (Shakespeare's *The Taming of the Shrew*, Jonson's *The Alchemist*, Heywood's *The English Traveller*) and one modern film (*A Funny Thing Happened on the Way to the Forum*). The intertextual dialogues among these adaptations can reveal as much as scholarly studies do about *Mostellaria*'s tone and stagecraft. Moving from the play's reception in drama and film, the companion closes by placing Tranio in a pantheon alongside a few other famous tricksters.

The *Postmortem* Scripts

Our earliest surviving manuscript of Plautus dates to the fourth or fifth century CE, some 500 years after his death. Prior to that, the roughly 130 scripts attributed to him had passed through unstable early transmission (a kind of theatrical beatification) before crystallizing into twenty-one definitively Plautine texts (their scholarly canonization). Unintended changes such as omissions, additions, transpositions, and errors inevitably creep into all texts copied by hand. Dramatic scripts circulating as actors' copies and not obligated by ritual to be verbatim are especially prone to changes both unintended and intended. They become post-theatrical transcripts of performances. Playwrights revise. With or without a playwright's input, troupes performing on multiple occasions will add, delete, or substitute material to satisfy the desires of varied audiences. After a playwright's death, theater practitioners can introduce changes to serve new audiences or venues. And while performers sometimes prefer to abridge scripts, readers often desire maximal texts preserving fuller or alternate versions. Our manuscripts of Plautus descend not directly from a pure authorial script but rather from an amalgam of actors' transcripts and copies for readers, assembled by scholars during the early Roman empire, to serve readers rather than performers.[1]

Our modern printed editions of Plautus depend upon four main manuscripts in two branches. One branch we call the Palatine Recension ("P"), represented in three manuscripts from the tenth and eleventh centuries. They provided the texts of Plautus in the early modern period. The other branch is the fourth or fifth-century Ambrosian Palimpsest (designated "A"), only rediscovered in the later eighteenth century and with excerpts first published in 1815 (the now almost illegible manuscript of Plautus had been reused to copy the Vulgate's Books of Kings [= 1, 2 Samuel and 1, 2 Kings]). Both branches descend from a common ancestor, most likely a codex for readers from the fourth century. That ancestor's text had already crystallized after passing through the period of instability described above. Thus, our manuscripts preserve a single conflated version of *Mostellaria* with a few variant readings rather than distinct versions, such as we see in our two alternate versions of *Lear* (original versus authorial revision), *Hamlet* (actors' memorial reconstruction versus text for readers), or Marlowe's *Faustus* (original versus later playwrights' revisions).[2] Unfortunately, for *Mostellaria* only about 300 lines survive from the mutilated Ambrosian Palimpsest.

The manuscripts of Plautus reveal traces of textual instability such as performance variants and errors of transcription. On every page, a modern printed Latin text of his plays will note variant readings found in the manuscripts, along with editors' conjectures for fixing obvious or suspected errors, omissions, and interpolations. Thanks to centuries of careful work by those editors, *Mostellaria*'s text is in satisfactory shape for reading and performing, aside from a few lines mutilated beyond repair that do not impede the flow of the action (e.g., traces of 1026a-e only found in A). Problems greater than the reading of an individual word are few and can be satisfactorily emended, including metrical or linguistic infelicities, uncertainty in the attribution of speakers (e.g., line 673), an occasional misplaced line (e.g., the devilishly hot 609a migrated to 666 in the manuscripts), or a line to be deleted on theatrical grounds (e.g., Theopropides' isolated interruption at 721a). The old man's name presents one significant point of contention because the manuscripts read "Theoropides," "Theuropides," and in two places "Theupropides." Most editors and translators prefer to print Theoprŏpides ("Son of the Prophet"), a real name that befits his superstitious nature. But Theorōpides ("Son of Spectator-Face") remains a possibility, and it emphasizes his role as the hoodwinked audience for Tranio's *ludi*.[3] With either name, irony undercuts his clairvoyance or his theatrical acumen.

Of special interest for performers is the presence of doublets, variant versions of a line or sequence. Doublets can serve as boundary markers for an expanded comic bit that a company may choose to omit. Let me give three examples. Theopropides' pun to Simo that he does not want to be "taken in" (*perducere*, swindled/given a house tour) appears twice in **Scene 7b**, at 816a-b and 845–6, and the second verses are identical. In between falls Tranio's mischievous metatheatrical foolery about the thick doorposts, sleeping door bolts, porridge-eating barbarians, and the painted crow mocking two vultures. Since those jokes require footnotes for full appreciation, a company may choose to cut the sequence to accelerate the pace, and the doublets mark the points for abridgment. If the sequence is retained, lines 845–6 steer the audience back to the story, akin to our phrase "as I was saying . . ."[4]

Scapha's comments at lines 224 and 247 are almost verbatim. If a troupe finds the grooming and eavesdropping **Scene 3a** "intolerably long," it can cut lines 224–44.[5] Such a cut not only accelerates the pace but also enriches the characterization of Scapha by suggesting that the cagey old woman suspects Philolaches' creepy presence. Her ability to sense his surveillance and asides, including death threats (212, 218–19,

223), motivates her abrupt change in advice to avoid a whipping administered by him rather than by Philematium (246). She then strives to earn the eavesdropper's applause, which he promises at line 260. While audience response to a given production will reveal whether this drag scene is dragging and demands abridgment, the manuscripts have preserved for readers the longer variant between Scapha's repeated lines.

In **Scene 5a**, line 425 also crops up between lines 411 and 412 in the Palatine manuscripts. The doublet marks a potential abridgment for lines 412–24, which contain Sphaerio's cameo. A troupe not needing Sphaerio's interruption to cover an actor's change from Philolaches into Theopropides can cut the lines and forgo their metatheatrical joke.

On the downside, doublets and other forms of textual instability prohibit reconstructing a single authorial Plautine text, and thus we should avoid pressing a given line's relevance to an original audience. On the upside, variants license a generous flexibility in revival productions. Unless members of a live audience have a text in hand, they will not notice expansions or abridgements in fast-paced Plautine farce.

Theatrical performances are evanescent events confined to a particular space and time. The manuscripts associated with performances are more portable and durable across space and time, allowing readers more leisurely and minute analysis of the language. The works of later Roman authors in non-dramatic genres, especially lyric and elegiac poetry, reveal close reading of and reaction to Plautine comedy.[6] The poems of Catullus, for example, construct a demimonde of *scorta* and boon companions enjoying wine, leisure, and song in scenarios translating Plautine comedy from stage to page.[7] In poem 5, for instance, Catullus invites his girlfriend Lesbia to live it up and make love (5.1) by giving him hundreds and thousands of kisses (5.7–10), valuing at a penny the disapproval of the *senes severiores* (the rather severe old men of comedy, 5.2–3) and confusing the gaze of any malevolent spectator (5.12). Amatory theme and diction closely recall the financial foreplay of Philolaches and Philematium in *Mostellaria*

Scene 3b (295–309). The Catullan reception of Plautus here casts Lesbia as meretricious and Catullus as prodigal. Equally, the reception compels us to reconsider characterization in *Mostellaria*. We may suspect that the physical, emotional, and moral bonds between Philolaches and Philematium have a complicated backstory, and the Catullan intertext forecasts that the Plautine couple will face a future stormier than the initial downpour of Love and Passion that unroofed Philolaches (162–5).

Three Early Modern English Reincarnations

Compared to other Latin authors, Plautus was not much read or copied in the Middle Ages because his archaic Latin mystified and the moral tenor of his plays was offensive to prevailing sensibilities. *Mostellaria* also fared poorly in the early Renaissance, in part because only the first eight alphabetically of his twenty comedies were known. *Mostellaria* resurfaced in the fifteenth century after the discovery of a manuscript containing the latter twelve in 1429; eventually the first complete edition of Plautus by Giorgio Merula was printed in 1472 in Venice.[8] After discovery of another manuscript in the sixteenth century, the German scholar Joachim Kammermeister (aka Camerarius) published an excellent complete edition (Basil, 1552). For *Mostellaria*, he shrewdly corrected the order of several scenes that the Palatine manuscripts had transposed.[9] Camerarius' edition became the basis for that of Denis Lambin (aka Lambinus; Paris, 1576), whose clean, easily read text in Roman rather than Italic type provides copious notes after each scene. Neither edition offers act divisions, a reminder that the divisions found in many modern editions and translations have no ancient authority. Instead, both editions mark the start of a new scene at someone's entry with headings listing the onstage characters. Scenes, not acts, are the compositional units in continuous performance without interludes. Since no English translation of *Mostellaria* appeared in print until the eighteenth century, any apparitions of the play derived from encounters with the Latin script, and Lambinus' was the more accessible edition of Plautus for schools, universities, and theater practitioners in early modern England.

Plautus had a profoundly transformative effect upon the dramaturgy of professional playwrights in early modern England. The following discussion of *Mostellaria*'s reception on the English stage offers not a contribution to the scholarly graveyard that is source criticism. Rather, it hopes to demonstrate a spectrum of strategies that three coeval playwrights used to appropriate ancient comedy, ranging from Shakespeare's incorporation of a pervasive but elusive Plautine substratum to Heywood's close translation of Plautus in circumscribed passages. Jonson's amalgamation of Plautine scenes and characters with other raw materials pursues a mercurial golden mean between rigid translation and wispy adaptation. All three dramatists offer lessons in how a modern playwright may, with varying success, *vortit barbare.*

Shakespeare proclaims his drama's Plautine priorities in one of his earliest efforts, **The Taming of the Shrew** (*c.* 1592). The play opens with a metatheatrical induction scene almost 300 lines long to establish the wastrel Christopher Sly as a spectator-eavesdropper of the ensuing play-within-a-play. After a fanfare of trumpets, the very first word of the inner play addresses a servant: "Tranio." The next scene introduces another servant, Grumio. And before that, in a surprising auditory ricochet, a suitor named Gremio. Nevertheless, Shakespeare's Tranio and Grumio bear scant resemblance to their Plautine namesakes, other than that his Grumio has his ears wrung (1.2.17 *stage direction*) and grumbles about beatings (4.1.2), and his Tranio is tricky, helps his young master pursue a love affair, and avoids punishment through an advocate's intervention (5.1.100–11).[10] Any material that source criticism might declare imported specifically from *Mostellaria*, such as the son Lucentio abandoning his studies for love (1.1.1–46) or his father Vincentio being locked out upon returning home (5.1), can with equal plausibility be attributed to the general stockpile of ancient Roman and Renaissance Italian comic tropes. This Shakespeare play does not engage with a single classical source in the kind of tight intertextual dialogue that we might expect from comparing *The Comedy of Errors* with Plautus' *Menaechmi*, or the later Roman plays with Plutarch's *Lives*. In those cases, Shakespeare worked with a text of the ancient author in hand. With its deceptions, disguises, eavesdropping, misunderstandings, love affairs, and parallel plots, *The Taming of the Shrew* is constructed according to general architectural principles of Roman New Comedy rather than by repurposing specific building blocks of character or plot found in *Mostellaria*.[11]

So why start a play with "Tranio"? If Hamlet marvels at an actor's passionate performance of tragedy by asking "What's Hecuba to him?" (*Hamlet*, 2.2.536), we might ask for comedy "What's Tranio to a Tudor?" While the names Tranio and Grumio offer practical advantages, they function as a symbol or synecdoche for Plautine farce and trickery. At a mundane level, Tranio and Grumio befit the play's Italian setting better than Tom, Dick, and Harry. At a sonic level, they offered Shakespeare useful metrical variation for working into iambic pentameter because they can be trisyllabic (GROO-me-O) or disyllabic (GROOM-yo). The lingering final "o" offers actors a variety of effects based on intonation such as impatient, teasing, or plaintive. The funny names resemble the contemporary clownish servants named Dromio in John Lyly's comedy *Mother Bombie* (*c.* 1590) and Shakespeare's own *The Comedy of Errors* (before 1594 and possibly before *Shrew*). But the real gain is that the names advertise Plautine farce as *Shrew*'s comic substratum. For tragedy in the Elizabethan era, Hecuba became a haunting symbol of the bereaved and vengeful mother. Her name functioned as a synecdoche or node to convey a meaningful nexus of plot, character, themes, and emotions.[12] Comedy lacked such mythical archetypes. Yet the saucy and distinctive names Tranio and Grumio clearly publicize Plautus rather than Terence, who gave bland and recycled names such as Parmeno and Syrus to several of his rather interchangeable slaves.[13] *The Taming of the Shrew* draws upon many stock features of Roman New Comedy both Plautine and Terentian, but Shakespeare's invocation of Tranio at the play's opening trumpets the predominance of Plautine elements that we have described earlier: outrageous characterization;

complicated deceits and disguises; boisterous and slapstick staging; music and bawdy bits; pervasive monologues, asides, and eavesdropping; intricate metatheater. For this reason, Polonius will invoke Plautus rather than Terence as the epitome of the comic spirit for actors: "Seneca cannot be too heavy, nor Plautus too light" (*Hamlet* 2.2.382–3).[14] Since reading and performing scenes of Plautus was a standard part of the Elizabethan grammar school curriculum, it is a fair bet that many members of Shakespeare's audience had met, and perhaps even a lucky few had played, the infamous Tranio.[15]

At the other end of the spectrum, Thomas Heywood offers a straightforward strategy of translating Tranio. Where Shakespeare may have vaguely remembered Tranio from his grammar school days, Heywood closely dissected his Latin text of *Mostellaria*. In the first four acts of the tragicomedy **The English Traveller** (1624 or 1627), Heywood interlards a serious plot with comic scenes cribbed from *Mostellaria*, sometimes with minor alterations in staging or topical allusions, more often with verbatim translations or glosses, and only occasionally with free composition. The comic subplot follows the familiar cast and exploits of Tranio (Reignald), Theopropides (old Lionel), Philolaches (young Lionel), and the rest, mostly renamed (Scapha keeps her name; Callidamates becomes simply "Rioter"). To the comic episodes Heywood adds two Gallants and a second prostitute to accompany Rioter, as well as the previous owner of the "haunted" house.

With a larger company of actors, Heywood's occasional innovations illuminate Plautus' economy in staging. For example, in Act 4 Scene 6, Heywood heightens the hubbub when, instead of Phaniscus and Pinacium revealing Tranio's deceits to Theopropides, we see onstage the house's previous owner accused of murder, the Grumio-figure, the Simo-figure, and the clown from the play's tragic story. This crowd ambushes Reignald, who climbs up the façade of old Lionel's house instead of an altar (4.6.208 *stage direction*).[16] Threatened with burning and shooting, Reignald blows a horn to summon young Lionel and the revelers to his rescue (4.6.253 *stage direction*), packing the stage with a dozen actors. Where Plautus avoided a scene reconciling duped father and prodigal son, Heywood composes a public reconciliation to satisfy a Caroline Christian audience, with the son and his friends on bended knees, the father weeping, and the son's promise to abandon his "wanton" girlfriend and her companions (4.6.284–6). Scapha's warning to Philematium about male inconstancy quoted above (pp. 29–30) finds sad fulfillment in Heywood as this happy ending entails renunciation of the woman. The Simo-figure rather than Rioter intercedes for Reignald's forgiveness, and all accept the clown's invitation to feast at the home figured in the tragic half.

Comparison with *Mostellaria* merits more detailed study.[17] Here I shall focus on the "ghost's" interruption in *Mostellaria* quoted in this companion's Playbill (pp. x–xi). Heywood cuts *Mostellaria*'s creaking door and, faithfully following the editions available to him, assigns to the old man the cry *Heu Tranio*! ("But Reignald!"):

Reignald

I entreat,

Keep further from the gate, and fly.

Old Lionel

Fly whither?

Why dost not thou fly too?

Reignald

What need I fear?

The Ghost and I are friends.

Old Lionel

But Reignald!

Reignald

Tush,

I nothing have deserved, nor aught transgressed;

I came not near the gate.

Old Lionel

To whom was that

Thou spakest?

Reignald

Was't you, sir, namèd me?

Now as I live, I thought the dead man called

To enquire for him that thundered at the gate
Which he so dearly paid for.

2.2.208–17

Heywood's close translation of his Plautine text requires the Reignald-actor to manufacture a misunderstanding with his scene partner. This staging generates less comic frenzy than having the trickster improvise an explanation for an unexpected shout from a reveler within (as in Plautus) or, as we shall see, shouts from an ally and a victim within (as in Jonson). Heywood's version reveals how simple translation of a Roman New Comic script onto the English stage yields muted comic effect.

Bolder is better. Ben Jonson's ***The Alchemist*** (1610), to some his comic masterpiece and to others an impenetrable tangle of disguises and esoterica, summons specters of *Mostellaria* in its opening scene and climax while updating elements to suit contemporary Jacobean preoccupations. Jonson exploits the theme of alchemy as a metapoetic boast that he takes the base materials of all his sources and transmutes them into comic gold, not unlike Plautus might claim to blend his own Greek and Italian raw materials.[18]

Left in charge of the master's house for months, Face (Jeremy the butler, in disguise) has formed a conspiracy with Subtle (a "cunning" con artist) and a prostitute (Doll Common) to swindle customers who believe that Subtle the Alchemist has discovered the Philosopher's Stone, a substance that transmutes all into gold. The play opens amid a rowdy quarrel in front of a house between Face and Subtle. The staging and abusive tones immediately recall Tranio and Grumio, though Jonson descends to saltier vulgarity from the opening verse ("I fart at thee!" … "Lick figs [hemorrhoids] out at my—" 1.1.1–3).[19] Associating the two playwrights reminds us that Plautus' language is relatively clean. Doll's intercession complicates the simpler, flatter Plautine staging of a duel by creating a triangle as when, for example, she resorts to violence both verbal and physical by taking Face's sword, smashing Subtle's beaker, and threatening to cut their throats (1.1.115 *stage direction*, 1.1.119). By reminding them of their business scheme ("venture tripartite," 1.1.136), Doll's forceful mediation broadens

Plautus' purely domestic concern—corrupting a young master—into a communal anxiety. There is no young master. The play skewers the corruption of Jacobean society with a parade of greedy, lustful citizens (clerk, merchant, knight, Puritans, others), as if Jonson channels an Aristophanic spirit through a New Comic medium.

To construct the play's climax, Jonson aggrandizes and complicates *Mostellaria*. Doll announces that master Lovewit, who had left town to escape an outbreak of the plague, has returned (4.7.108–9). Taking charge, Face orders his co-conspirators to go inside the house, "be silent; not a word, if he call or knock" (4.7.119), and pack up the loot. The mercurial Face will resume his identity as Jeremy, drive off Lovewit for the day (4.7.124), and the three will rendezvous tomorrow to divide the booty. Locked out and banging on the door, Lovewit learns from six neighbors that day and night a diverse clientele has entered the house (5.2.1–6), as Theopropides had learned from Phaniscus and Pinacium. The neighbors claim that Jeremy has been absent for weeks, and that they heard spooky noises (5.2.33, 36–7). Jeremy emerges to explain that he has been absent and the house locked up for fumigation after fear of plague from an infected feline (5.2.4–14). Fear of a real and deadly Jacobean epidemic in that very year replaces *Mostellaria*'s funny, fictitious haunting. Jeremy denies the neighbors' claims, and Lovewit believes his servant. But revelation looms as the defrauded customers return. Jeremy turns to address the audience: "What shall I do? / "Nothing is more wretched than a guilty conscience." (5.2.46–7). The aphorism quotes *Mostellaria* line 544 (though the sentiment is common enough), possibly to footnote the Plautine intertext in preparation for the upcoming climax.

Jeremy and Lovewit rebuff the fraud victims until the clerk, left bound and gagged awaiting a female visitor inside the house's privy (yuck!), chews through his gag and yelps for help. Jeremy juggles audiences in telling Lovewit that the noises offstage are spirits, making asides to the theatergoers, and shushing both victim and conspirator inside the house. We appreciate Jonson's bold experimentation in classical reception when we compare his adaptation to the Plautine passage quoted in this companion's Playbill and Heywood's translation:

Clerk (*cries out within*)
Master Captain! Master Doctor!
Lovewit
Who's that?
Jeremy (*aside to us*)
Our clerk within, that I forgot. (*to Lovewit*) I know not, sir.
Clerk (*within*)
For God's sake, when will Her Grace be at leisure?
Jeremy (*to Lovewit*)
Ha!
Illusions, some spirit o'the air! (*aside to us*) His gag is melted,
And now he sets out the throat.
Clerk (*within*)
I am almost stifled.
Jeremy (*aside to Clerk within*)
Would you were altogether!
Lovewit
'Tis i'the house.
Ha! List!
Jeremy
Believe it, sir, i'the air.
Lovewit
Peace, you—
Clerk (*within*)
Mine aunt's Grace does not use me well.
Subtle (*within, to Clerk*)
You fool,
Peace, you'll mar all!
Jeremy (*through the keyhole to Subtle*)
Or you will else, you rogue!
Lovewit
Oh, is it so? Then you converse with spirits!
Come, sir. No more o'your tricks, good Jeremy.
The truth, the shortest way.

5.3.63–74; some stage directions added to Jonson's

Jonson moves a memorable highlight from *Mostellaria*'s middle—Tranio using a voice from inside the "haunted" house to drive off Theopropides—and magnified its prominence by making it the climax that prompts Jeremy's confession and a reconciliation. The passage demonstrates Jonson's exquisite feel for Plautine stagecraft and the importance of line attribution in a script. The early modern editions of *Mostellaria* assigned to Theopropides the cry *Heu Tranio*! (Yo! Tranio!, 515), as we saw with Heywood ("But Reignald!"). Modern editions of Plautus follow a suggestion by F. Rost from 1824 in assigning the outburst to a reveler inside the house. Rost's attribution offers superior comedic effect by requiring Tranio to manipulate characters on both sides of the portal. Jonson intuited that the shouts of Subtle and the clerk emanating from behind the façade, and Face backtalking through the keyhole, raise the dramatic stakes of handling two at a time (cf. p. 74) to a supreme level. Through comparative analysis of one passage, we can perceive how smaller factors such as textual instability, asides to the audience, and freer adaptation versus closer translation encapsulate larger conclusions about the tone and stagecraft of dramatic artists. Heywood's faithful translation of Plautus produces less vivacious comedy than Jonson's bolder ventures into *vortere*.

Caught but resourceful, Jeremy obtains his master's pardon with bridal bribery: Lovewit can wed a rich widow (Dame Pliant, a swindled victim inside the house) if he will don a disguise. Lovewit is no theatrically obtuse Theopropides, for he joins Jeremy's matchmaking play-within-a-play (5.3.85–91) and returns boasting that he consummated the union (5.5.56–8). As with Theopropides, the master's motivation is financial. The play ends in an almost Menandrean tone, with Dame Pliant's brother promising Lovewit a hefty dowry to seal the marriage bond, the men accepting their status as brothers-in-law, and adjournment to celebrate inside (5.5.136–46). To conclude, Lovewit addresses the audience directly to express contentment with his bride's wealth and to fulfill the promise of his name by granting indulgence to his "servant's wit" (5.5.146–57). In a nifty variation on Plautus' final scene, Jeremy/Face delivers a metatheatrical speech to end the show, in which he asks forgiveness from the paying spectators and invites them to subsequent feasts (i.e., to purchase tickets to another performance full of skullduggery).

Shakespeare, Heywood, and Jonson typify the range of strategies by which early modern English playwrights conjure up the spirit of Roman New Comedy and bend it to new purposes and contexts. Unlike the early modern mythographers who merely transmitted narratives of classical myth as antiquarians, these playwrights creatively adapt classical models to produce new, hybrid forms of drama. They *vortunt barbare* and thereby resemble Plautus in his handling of Greek New Comedy. This is one reason that scholars have moved away from speaking of the classical tradition (literally "handing over"), whereby ancient works influence (literally "pour into") later artists, as if the later artists were passive vessels or possessed bodies. We now prefer to speak of classical reception, which stresses the innovative activities of modern artists to establish mutually enriching dialogues across centuries and cultures.

A Funny Thing Happened on the Way to the Forum

Plays go in and out of vogue, and *Mostellaria* perhaps has fallen out of favor. For example, we have no recent school editions with English commentary, and generally less scholarship on this play than on others. Most likely someone's only acquaintance with *Mostellaria* would come in disguise through *A Funny Thing Happened on the Way to the Forum.* With catchy music and lyrics by Stephen Sondheim and a snappy, bawdy, pun-filled book by Burt Shevelove and Larry Gelbart, the 1962 Broadway play won Tony Awards for Best Musical, Best Actor, Best Supporting Actor, Best Book, and Best Director. The 1966 film version, directed by Richard Lester and screenplay by Melvin Frank and Michael Pertwee, parades a cast of the era's comic stars, including Zero Mostel as the clever slave Pseudolus and Buster Keaton in his final film as old father Erronius. It won the Academy Award for Best Adapted Score and earned a Golden Globe nomination for best film. The play has enjoyed revival productions on major stages (e.g., the 1996–1997 Broadway run featured as Pseudolus Nathan Lane, then Whoopi Goldberg, then David Alan Grier) and in local companies.

A Funny Thing seamlessly interweaves characters and plots from several Plautine comedies, including *Pseudolus, Mostellaria, Miles Gloriosus, Casina,* and *Curculio.*[20] *Mostellaria* contributes the scheme of switching houses and tricking the old father with a ghost story. Pseudolus and the pimp next door agree to swap identities and households, and when Erronius returns from years abroad, he learns that his house is "haunted as the day is long." As the superstitious Erronius runs seven times around the Seven Hills of Rome, Pseudolus invents other plots to help his hapless and infatuated young master free his beloved girl. In the end, Pseudolus not only escapes punishment but even obtains his freedom.

A Funny Thing demonstrates the almost algebraic nature of Roman New Comedy, whereby stock characters and formulaic plots permit substitutions within individual scenes that still yield valid, predictable, and satisfying comic endings. For example, since a pimp owns one of the three houses in *A Funny Thing*, the plot function of *Mostellaria*'s housing scam between Theopropides and Simo can be transferred and divided among the pimp, Erronius, and Senex (the Simo-figure). The pimp's occupation adds a slew of variables from comedies that feature *meretrices*. The presence of prostitutes inside the young lover's house ("for a sit-down orgy for fourteen") multiplies exponentially the scene of debauchery in *Mostellaria* and the clever slave's challenge to conceal it all. Or again, in *A Funny Thing* old Erronius is father not of the young lover, who is the son of Senex, but of the beloved virgin courtesan stolen long ago by filthy pirates. That change introduces plot elements from Roman comedies culminating in joyful family reunions.

Through such substitutions, Shevelove and Gelbart multiply the madcap complexity of Plautine plots. They out-Plautus Plautus. In doing so, they continued the New Comic tradition of one-upmanship through interweaving plots and characters from different plays. We believe that Plautus did so to embroider his Greek models; Terence boasts that he followed Plautus' practice by inserting scenes from different Greek scripts; Shakespeare's *The Comedy of Errors* splices a scene and second set of doppelgängers from *Amphitruo* into the text of *Menaechmi*; Jonson's *The Case is Altered* fuses *Captivi* and *Aulularia*; Heywood's *The English Traveller* stitches together *Mostellaria* and a tragedy; and so on.[21]

Fuller appreciation of these comedies comes through a study of confluence or triangulation among several plays rather than reading forwards or backwards between *Mostellaria* and a single later incarnation. For instance, we can posit *The Alchemist* as an intermediary between *Mostellaria* and *A Funny Thing* for a few suggestive details about pornography and potions. We may wonder at *A Funny Thing*'s gratuitous pornographic detail that the slave-in-charge Hysterium "has secreted in his cubicle Rome's most extensive collection of erotic pottery" (suggestively mimed by Pseudolus). We find no corresponding concept in Plautus (though Tranio does sleep with prostitutes). But in *The Alchemist*, Lovewit guesses that his butler Jeremy attracts visitors by displaying tapestries with "bawdy pictures" such as "The knight's courser covering [copulating with] the parson's mare, / The boy of six year old with the great thing [penis]" (5.1.21–4). Lovewit eventually discovers in his home "A few cracked pots, and glasses . . . And 'Madam with a dildo' writ o'the walls" (5.5.40–2). While Pompeiian wall paintings might have inspired the general use of background frescoes in *A Funny Thing*, the placement of erotic artworks specifically in Hysterium's room invites actors and audiences to consider the degree to which the film imported salacious backstories from Jonson rather than Roman New Comedy.

The concoction and confusion of potions in *A Funny Thing* is utterly foreign to Plautus but quite familiar in early modern English theater (e.g., *Romeo and Juliet*, *Hamlet*). In *A Funny Thing*, we see a busy kitchen in which Pseudolus uses a secret spell to concoct a sleeping potion (including a cup of mare's sweat). He stole the spell from Hysterium, the loyal majordomo who chooses to conspire with Pseudolus to deceive their master. The potion and conspiracy have no connection to *Mostellaria*, for Tranio the majordomo is no apothecary and the loyal slave Grumio opposes him. *The Alchemist* provides a theatrical emulsifier as the con man Subtle and the butler Jeremy/Face conspire to concoct their snake oil. Through triangulation, we see how Hysterium bears little resemblance to Tranio or the cowherd Grumio, but his unreliable and conflicted loyalty does resemble that of Jeremy/Face in *The Alchemist*. Jonson uses alchemy as a metaphor for a playwright mixing raw materials. Shevelove, Gelbart, and Frank tap into that metaphor at both superficial and deep levels. *A Funny Thing*'s confusion of a sleeping potion and an aphrodisiac is not just wacky: it winks at the conflation of tragic and comic genres in a way that recalls Heywood's *The English Traveller*. A sleeping potion in comedy proves harmless, in tragedy fatal. Though *senex* may not agree, *A Funny Thing* serves up bawdy comedy tonight.

For many people, *A Funny Thing* offers the most accessible reincarnation of the comic techniques and spirit of Plautus. Yet for all its exuberant fun and critical acclaim, some moral and political elements disturbing to modern audiences must not be brushed aside. In the film version, Richard Lester sought to critique sanitized and idealized images of Rome with scenes whose "sordid" images undercut the cheery dialogue and lyrics.[22] The film's pervasive objectification of women deserves censure, and its callous treatment of slaves for laughs (e.g., the sale of a plump female slave known as "The Breeder") makes any insouciant use of it impossible. With their focus on systemic structures rather than individuals, such modern objections differ from the moral qualms of the Middle Ages and early modern period, which focused on exorcizing from the curriculum the vicious examples of Plautine pimps, prostitutes, and debauched young men. Throughout history, many people have distrusted the ostracizing elements of laughter that objectifies or belittles.[23] With inclusivity as a desirable (if not essential) goal in an often cruel and divided world, we may now value comedies that pursue congenial laughter through incongruities and reconciliations rather than through derisive scapegoating or objectification. *A Funny Thing* ends by celebrating friendship, marriage, family reunion, and freedom without the discordant tones found in comedies that banish rather than integrate outsiders. But can or should a line from *A Funny Thing*'s closing song, "morals tomorrow, comedy tonight!" excuse any amorality, parody, and social commentary in a 1960's American renovation of Plautus? Such questions can make the film good to think with rather than simply an aesthetic object.

Moderns revive or appropriate ancient texts to articulate contemporary preoccupations, and ancient plays drift into and out of vogue. If *Mostellaria* is currently understudied and underperformed, perhaps discomfort with the unpalatable or strange social elements in Chapter 2 has overshadowed the joyous theatrical features of Chapter 3. Or perhaps we as classicists and dramaturgs have failed to answer the fundamental question: "why read or stage this play now?" Teachers to their students, and directors to their audiences and boards, feel an urgency to demonstrate that an investment of time and money will provide a payoff beyond two hours of amusement. Perhaps it need not be so. But for someone teaching a class or writing an essay for a theater's playbill, I would submit that *Mostellaria*'s Roman themes are not so alien to (e.g.) contemporary America: venture capitalism and real estate speculation; paranormal activity; prodigal young men lacking parental supervision; the exploitation of women; tensions between rural and urban counties; the incorporation or rejection of foreign elements; the legacies of our postcolonial and slave-owning past. Just as instructors and theater companies must weigh the pros and cons of teaching and performing (e.g.) *The Taming of the Shrew* or *Othello*, individuals need to address, though not necessarily adjudicate, the positives and negatives of choosing this play now from the canon of ancient comedy. Ultimately, I would hope that celebration of Tranio's ingenuity can overcome or circumvent any obstacles and reservations.

Tranio Trickster

As a *servus callidus*, Roman New Comedy's stock clever slave, Tranio is an ancestor of theatrical tricksters rather than fools or clowns. That is, he is not a witty fool such as Lear's Fool, whose banter speaks truth to power and reveals royal folly with impunity. Nor is he a clown such as Dromio in *The Comedy of Errors*, whose jokes and slapstick amuse without bite. Fools and clowns are seldom the creators of elaborate metatheatrical plots. Nor is Tranio a rogue like Subtle and Doll in Jonson's *The Alchemist*, a "character who is detached from a settled mode of existence, depends on his wit and ruthlessness for his survival, and perpetrates crimes rather than mere practical jokes."[24] Like other Plautine clever slaves, Tranio is an architect of deceit whose fabrications temporarily subvert aspects of the established order without dismantling the order.

If we look to isolate direct theatrical descendants of Tranio we will be disappointed, because rarely do we find compelling evidence to identify him rather than some other Plautine trickster as the model. Instead, we can broaden our search from receptions to seek his siblings among tricksters found throughout world folklore and myth. I would like to draw from Lewis Hyde's *Trickster Makes This World* (1999), which offers a delightful and brisk tour of tricksters in nature, myth, and art. Hyde surveys such seemingly disparate beings as bacteria and octopuses, Coyote and Raven, Krishna and Eshu, Frederick Douglass and Pablo Picasso as avatars for the cunning, creative, rebellious, and transformative powers of comic mischief. Hyde's use of the *Homeric Hymn to Hermes* as a hermeneutic guide for finding connections justifies using the book in a study of ancient comedy, even though Hyde does not examine Roman tricksters or tricksters in drama. Indeed, those omissions leave an open invitation to readers to apply the book's observations to theatrical tricksters such as Tranio.[25]

Hyde's chapters reveal tricksters driven by appetite, undone by their own wits, opportunistic and improvisatory with lucky finds, shameless in their amorality, and joyfully operating at the thresholds and joints of society. Many of those features illuminate Tranio's activities, but I shall focus on that last aspect, how Tranio resembles Hermes and other tricksters as liminal figures that control thresholds.

Hermes is a god of movement through, around, or between barriers, the one who resourcefully finds a way (Greek *poros*) out of paralyzing perplexity (*aporia*). He is the god of the hinges, of transitions, transactions, transformations, and such.[26] No staging in Plautus focuses our attention on facades and thresholds as emphatically as *Mostellaria*. Other plays feature an isolated lockout scene, but *Mostellaria* makes Tranio's control of portals paramount. He drives off Grumio in the opening scene and then cloisters the revelers who had spilled into the street during his absence. With a special key brought to him by his assistant Sphaerio in a cameo, we watch Tranio double lock the house so that no one can exit and no one can enter. Tranio performs like the magician on stage, bound by locks before our eyes and having only wit and sleight of hand to escape his self-imposed trap. In asides to the audience, Tranio expresses his *aporia* to raise the suspense. But, like a magician, he finds a *poros* and escapes with his assistants through the *angiportus*.

Like Hermes, Tranio even manipulates the threshold between the living and the dead.[27] In Scene 5a, he conjures up a ghost that drives Theopropides down to Acheron still living. In Scene 7b, he frames the terms by which Theopropides crosses over into Simo's house. After critiquing Simo's doorposts and confounding the old men with a phantasmagorical painting of the carrion crow mocking two carrion vultures, Tranio the psychopomp leads Theopropides past a dog (Cerberus?) into Simo's home. At the play's conclusion, Tranio occupies an altar, a tangible portal between the profane and the sacred.

Mostellaria's ending will not satisfy those who prefer a neat and joyful resolution such as the (re)establishment of domestic harmony in Menander, or Pseudolus earning his freedom in *A Funny Thing*. But those teleological resolutions prioritize linear plot over character. *Mostellaria* goes sideways more often than forward. The play's ending—with Tranio perched on the altar and promising more mischief tomorrow—signifies the choice of the trickster figure to remain at the margins, crossroads, or threshold. Hyde's observation fits (1999: 220):

> From the edge of a group or the threshold of a house there are only a few ways a trickster can move: he can come inside, he can leave entirely, or he can stay exactly where he started, resisting all attempts to civilize or exile. From the trickster's point of view, this last, staying on the threshold, must be the ideal type; it gives us the plot that never resolves itself, the endlessly strung-together Coyote tales . . .

Plautus keeps Tranio on the threshold, and Tranio seems happy with the "pleasures of liminality."[28] He is neither incorporated into the citizen body as a manumitted slave nor exiled to the rural chain gang; rather, he continues as Theopropides' enslaved and mistrusted majordomo, a wily outsider inside the house, uniquely positioned to continue his comic hijinks in ways unimaginable for son Philolaches, rustic Grumio, or dependent Philematium. Only by remaining on the threshold can Tranio continue to critique and subvert the status quo tomorrow.

Tranio's continuation in a liminal status distinguishes him from his later dramatic reincarnations in Jeremy and Reignald, who seek forgiveness and reintegration. The contrast is most striking in Heywood's resolution to the conflict in *The English Traveller*:

Old Lionel

O thou crafty wag-string,
And couldst thou thus delude me? But we are friends.
[. . .]
Well, Reignald—but no more.

Reignald

I was the fox,
But I from henceforth will no more the cox-
Comb put upon your pate.

4.6.319–20, 325–7

After the deluding, master and servant become friends, an impossibility for Tranio and Theopropides. Reignald renounces his very identity as a trickster, for "Reignald" connotes the wily fox (cf. French *renard*).

Tranio's contentment with the perilous pleasures of liminality also distinguishes him from trickster figures such as Olympian Hermes or liberated Frederick Douglass, whose energetic and cunning intelligence permanently changes their status and modifies the established order. The former uses deceit to rise from birth in a cave to install himself among the Olympians as Zeus' mischievous but loyal lackey. The latter uses some techniques of the trickster to cross boundaries between the races and then vigorously advocate to help dismantle those impediments to others.[29]

A trickster remaining in liminal status comes at a price for the trickster but ensures our continuing entertainment. However much we celebrate Tranio's wit, the assessment of N. J. Lowe rings true: Tranio is "Plautus's most hopeless slave hero" because his deceptions of "ever more desperate and flimsy improvisations" are "doomed from the start."[30] Tranio's ghost story and housing swindle have no hope of lasting success. Part of the fun watching *Mostellaria* is an expectation that Tranio's latest scheme will end in *failure* rather than success, and thereby spawn another scheme. To my mind, Native America's Coyote provides the most illuminating folkloric trickster parallel for Tranio. Through his own cleverness, Coyote gets into trouble, survives a scrape, and proceeds to initiate his next challenge. When compared with the Loony Tunes barbarizations of folkloric tricksters, Tranio resembles less the triumphant Bugs Bunny than the truly harebrained and indestructible Wile E. Coyote with his latest shipment of rocket-propelled ACME products.

The best-case scenario for Tranio is only a temporary reprieve, and so the play simply stops with Tranio's promise to resume more mischief tomorrow and accept a double dose of Theopropides' revenge (1179). Enjoying *Mostellaria*'s festive non-teleological farce, we wonder what device Tranio will try in the next scene, or even, with a different name but the same mask, tomorrow.

Appendix 1: Pliny's "Haunted House" (Letter 7.27.5–11)

There was in Athens a house spacious and roomy but infamous and plagued. Throughout the stillness of the night, the clanking of iron and, if you were to listen more closely, the rattling of chains would echo, at first farther off, then from very close. Soon a ghost [*idolon*] would appear, an old man worn out by emaciation and filth, with a shaggy beard, bristling hair; it kept dragging the fetters on its feet and shaking the shackles on its wrists. So, the residents were kept awake through dismal and dreadful nights by fear. Sickness and, with their terror growing, death followed sleep deprivation. For in daytime too, even though the ghost [*imago*] had vanished, the memory of the ghost would drift before their eyes, and the horror lingered longer than the source of horror. Therefore, the house was deserted and condemned to vacancy and entirely abandoned to that ghost [*monstrum*]. But it was advertised in case someone ignorant of so great a curse would want to buy or lease it.

The philosopher Athenodorus comes to Athens. He reads the advertisement and when he hears the price, because the cheap rate is suspicious, asks around. He's told everything, and nevertheless, in fact even more, he rents it. When twilight comes, he orders his bed to be prepared in the front part of the house; he demands writing tablets, a pen, and a lamp; he dismisses all his people to the interior rooms. He focuses his willpower, eyes, and hand on writing, so that his idle mind would not conjure up phantom noises and empty fears for itself. At first, like everywhere else, silence of the night. Then iron clanging, chains dragging. He doesn't raise his eyes, doesn't drop his pen, but he strengthens his willpower and shields his ears. Then the racket increases, approaches, and sounds now like it's on the threshold, now like it's inside. He looks back, sees it, and recognizes the ghost [*effigies*] described to him. It was standing and gesturing with its finger like someone beckoning. He, in return, signals with his hand that it should wait a little and pays attention to his wax tablets and pen. It kept jangling the chains over his head while he's writing. He looks back again; it's gesturing the same as before; and without delay he picks up the lamp and follows. It was walking with a heavy step, as if burdened with chains. After it veered off into the house's courtyard, it suddenly dissolved and deserted its companion. He, deserted, marks the spot with weeds and shredded leaves.

On the next day, he goes to the magistrates, advises them to order that spot to be dug up. Bones are found entwined and entangled with chains. The body, rotted by age and the soil, had left the bones bare and gnawed by the chains. The bones are collected and buried at public expense. The house afterwards was free of the *Manes* laid to rest with proper ceremony.

Appendix 2: A Doubling Chart

Line numbers mark when a character enters, exits, and remains present throughout a scene (+).

Scene and lines	Actor 1 Tranio	Actor 2 Philolaches Theopropides	Actor 3 Philematium Pinacium	Actor 4 Scapha Delphium Phaniscus	Actor 5 Callidamates Simo
Scene 1 (1–83) [& Grumio 1–83]	6–75				
Scene 2 (84–156)		Ph:84 +			
Scene 3a (157–247)		+	Ph:157 +	Sc:157 +	
Scene 3b (248–312)		+	+	+ 294	
Scene 4a (313–347)		+	+	De:313 +	Ca:313 +
Scene 4b (348–408)	348	+ 406	+ 398 (silent)	+ 398	+ 387
Scene 5a (409–531) [& Sphaerio 419–426]	+	Th:431–528			
Scene 5b (532–654) [& Misargyrides 532–654]	+	Th:541 +			
Scene 5c (655–689)	+	+			
Scene 6a (690–746)	+	+ (silent)			Si:690 +
Scene 6b (747–782)	+	+ (silent)			+
Scene 7a (783–804)	+	+			+ (silent)
Scene 7b (805–857)	+ 857	+ 857			+ 853
Scene 8a (858–884)				Ph:858 +	
Scene 8b (885–903)			Pi:885 +	+	
Scene 9a (904–932)	904–932	Th:904 +	+ (silent)	+ (silent)	
Scene 9b (933–992)		+	+ 992	+ 992	
Scene 10 (993–1040)		+1040			Si:993–1040
Scene 11a (1041–1121)	1041 +	Th:1064 +			
Scene 11b (1122–1181)	+	+			Ca:1122 +

The table is illustrative rather than definitive for how a company with five speaking actors might cast the play based upon the following considerations:

1. The single-scene roles of Grumio and Misargyrides are independent and can be assigned to any of Actors 3–5. Any of Actors 3–5 can pop out for Sphaerio's cameo.

2. Scene 4b establishes the minimum requirement of five speaking actors. Tranio's arrival requires five speakers onstage concurrently at 344–8. (Philematium does not speak in 4b, but her presence is confirmed at 397.)
3. Twenty lines provide sufficient cover for an actor changing masks and costumes and moving backstage. For examples, the actor playing Philolaches exits through his doorway at 406 and enters from the wing as Theopropides at 431; the actor playing Scapha exits into the house at 294 and enters as Delphium from the wing at 313.

Appendix 3: Character Line Counts

Character	Iambic senarii (unaccompanied)	Cantica (mixed meters)	Trochaic + iambic septenarii	Total line count
Tranio	230	35	140	405
Theopropides	95	10	110	215
Philolaches		75	45 + 30	150
Simo	30	40	10	80
Scapha			25 + 40	65
Phaniscus		30	30	60
Grumio	55			55
Callidamates		20	30	50
Philematium		5	15 + 20	40
Misargyrides	35			35
Pinacium		15	5	20
Delphium		10	5	15
Sphaerio	3			3
	448	240	505	1193

Figures are intended to give a notion of workload in various meters and total line counts, both to explore possible ancient role doubling and to aid casting a modern show based upon an actor's vocal talent or comfort with large or small parts. Note that if the same actor plays Philolaches and Theopropides, that actor and the Tranio-actor will carry the three largest roles with nearly two-thirds of all lines.

Leaving aside lines mutilated or doubtfully assigned in the manuscripts, shared lines render the totals approximate. Line 641 exemplifies the impossibility of precise totals: Theo: *qui scire possum?* Tra: *uah!* Theo: *quid est?* Tra: *ne me roga.* I counted a half line apiece, but one could argue for one line apiece because both actors must speak, or even more since each actor must pick up two cues. Since the counts are only approximations, I have rounded totals to fives and tens (hence my composite line count of 1193 exceeds the play's received text of 1181).

Appendix 4: A Selective Chronology

Important ancient persons and events referred to in the text. All dates BCE.

Social, Political, Military	**Theatrical, Literary**
Fourth century-133 "Middle Republic" of Roman history	371–287 Theophrastus c. 362–262 Philemon
356–323 Alexander the Great 264–241 First Punic War 218–201 Second Punic War (Hannibal)	c. 350–c.290 Diphilus c.342–c.290 Menander 240 Livius Andronicus stages a play
c.212 introduction of denarius coinage	c.260–201 Naevius (first play in 235)
	c.254–184 Plautus 239–169 Ennius
197 Spanish provinces organized	234–149 Cato the Elder
195 repeal of *lex Oppia* (sumptuary law on female luxury)	c.220–167 Caecilius Statius 200 *Stichus*
193 first public porticoes in Rome	194 seats in theater reserved for senators
193–191 credit crisis, fines on usurers	191 *Pseudolus*
187 Gn. Manlius Vulso's triumph	
184 Cato Censor	185–159 Terence (plays 166–160)
182 *lex Orchia* (sumptuary law on dining)	160s Cato writes *Origines, de Agricultura*

161 *lex Fannia* (sumptuary law on dining)	167 Polybius in Rome, begins writing his history of Rome covering 220–167
160 funeral of L. Aemilius Paullus	

Notes

Chapter 1

1 Moore (2012) uses *Mostellaria* to introduce the typical features of Plautus.

2 These early works survive only in fragments quoted by later authors. Authors of tragedies include Naevius and Ennius. Ennius likely began composing his *Annales*—the pathbreaking Latin epic in hexameters—in the late 180s BCE. Roman historians writing in Greek started with Fabius Pictor *c.* 200. Cato likely began composition of his *Origines*, the first Italian history in Latin, in the 160s but likely had already circulated his political oratory in writing. For judicious surveys of these and other Latin authors, see Conte (1994) and Gratwick (1982). Feeney (2016) explores the ideology and practices enabling the translation project.

3 Braden, Cummings and Gillespie (2011).

4 Text and translation of Menander in Arnott (1979–2000); topical studies in Sommerstein (2014).

5 On Diphilus and Philemon in context, see Scafuro (2014); Olson (2007) for thematically arranged text and translation of comic fragments.

6 The nasal *n* in *monstrum* drops out in the compound *Mostellaria* (cf. *cos.* as abbreviation for *consul*). Since at least two other Greek playwrights wrote a *Phasma*, we cannot assume that Philemon's play was Plautus' model. Notably, the Roman imperial grammarian Festus twice quotes from *Mostellaria*, calling the play *Phasma*. See de Melo (2011: 307–8).

7 Cf. Anderson (1993: 30–59).

8 Handley (1968: 18). Cf. Barsby (1986: 140): "Menander's characterisation is complex, subtle, and realistic, Plautus' is simple, bold, and comic; Menander portrays the character sympathetically from inside, Plautus rather stands outside and risks destroying the credibility of the character for a laugh." Cf. especially Goldberg (1990), Anderson (1993: 3–29), Barbiero (2016).

9 Cf. Goldberg on Terence's Menandrean *Andria*: Terence's plays have "plenty in them to make audiences smile and nod, but not so much to make them hoot and holler. His texts are markedly austere, with few of the show-stopping effects typical of Plautine comedy." (2019: 14–15).

10 Cf. Wright (1974), de Melo (2014). Terence, writing a full generation after Plautus, overturns or attenuates some elements of that stylistic unity.

11 Gellius (*Attic Nights* 15.24) preserves a top ten ranking of Roman comic poets by a scholar named Volcacius Sedigitus in which Caecilius holds first place, Plautus second, and Naevius third. Terence takes sixth, Ennius tenth, and Livius Andronicus does not place.

12 Cf. Manuwald (2011: 169–77), Petrides (2014), Panayotakis (2019).

13 Cf. Schironi (2013) on the lack of continuity from the controlling clever slave in Plautus to the controlled, buffoonish *zanni* in commedia dell'arte.

14 Gellius 2.23.12: *alia nescioqua mimica inculcavit*; cf. Manuwald (2011: 178–83).

15 Cf. Moore (2020), Fontaine (2014). Stärk (1991) proposes that Plautus extensively renovated the Greek model of *Mostellaria* by inserting routines of impromptu, Italian origin.

16 Connors (2004) explores Plautine adaptation as a kind of monkey business.

17 Cf. Janka (2004) on some parallels and inversions of characterization and theme.

18 Leo (1913: 110–11) traces Grumio's Homeric portrayal to Philemon. Even if *Mostellaria*'s Odyssean elements derive from Philemon, those elements gain new meaning within the Roman reception of Homer.

19 Cf. Segal (1987: 15–21) on Plautine sons expressing rebellious wishes against parental authority.

20 James (2020).

21 Cf. Anderson (1993: 60–87) on lovers upstaged in other Plautine plays.

22 Cf. Segal's thesis that Plautus offers a Greek holiday for the Roman super ego (1987: 13).

23 If *Mostellaria* had repeat performances during a festival, "tomorrow" could be literally true. See pp. 58–9 on the crapulent Callidamates as a spoof of the *deus ex machina* and pp. 90–2 on *Mostellaria*'s non-teleological conclusion.

24 Cf. Gruen (1992: 31): "The Greeks imposed the Trojan legend upon the West as a form of Hellenic cultural imperialism, only to see it appropriated by the westerner to define and convey a Roman cultural identity." Plautus' gleeful appropriation and transformation of his Greek models makes visible and risible this kind of cultural Jiu Jitsu.

25 Cf. Feeney (2016: 54–5), McElduff (2013: 43–55).

26 Telò (2019: 49–55; quotation on 51); cf. Papaioannou (2016: 187–94), McElduff (2013: 66–73).
27 Slater (2000: esp. 139–47).
28 To be clear, *Mostellaria* does not compare Tranio to Ulysses, probably because the challenge facing Tranio differs fundamentally from that facing Chrysalus and Pseudolus. They use deceit, disguise, and the gift of gab to plunder the opposition, much as Ulysses the Sacker of Cities captured the Trojan citadel. In contrast, Tranio is besieged and protecting the booty inside the house (1048). He has no opportunity to triumph other than temporarily warding off his master. Cf. Philippides (1999) on *Mostellaria* as a sequence of sieges.
29 Leach (1969: 322–7) demonstrates the play's thematic emphasis on *exemplum* and *simulacrum*. Simo's very name connotes "monkey-man" or "translator/imitator."
30 Cf. Gowers (1993: 54) on *pultiphagus* signifying "Roman."

Chapter 2

1 The funeral celebrations of T. Quinctius Flamininus in 174 BCE presented banquets, plays, and gladiators. Those of L. Aemilius Paullus in 160 included two comedies of Terence, and, according to the prologue of *Hecyra*, the rumor of a gladiatorial show interrupted that play's performance. Roman dramatic performances in festivals would precede or follow feasting upon sacrificial animals freshly butchered. For analogous juxtapositions of comedy and blood sport, cf. early modern London where theaters stood near a ring for bearbaiting, such that "bearbaiting and theater were culturally isomorphic events" (Dickey 1991), or bullfighting rings near museums and theaters today.
2 Cf. Moore (1991), Goldberg (2018), Hanses (2020a), Gellar-Goad (2021: 104–16).
3 See Papaioannou (2020) on the blended Greek and Roman topography.
4 Cf. Gruen (1990: 124–57; 2014), Germany (2019). Cicero (*de Republica* 4.10.11) contrasts Aristophanic political topicality with Plautine silence.
5 The play's three references to a *porticus* (756, 908, 910; the only such references in Plautus) could allude to the building of Rome's first public

porticoes in 193 (Livy 35.10.12), and some lines in the moneylender's scene could relate to a credit crisis in the later 190s (see p. 35); cf. Buck (1940: 85–6).

6 Plautus lived within the period commonly termed the "Middle Republic." Polybius, our best primary source for the era, frames the fifty-three-year period of 220–167 BCE as a unit based upon external warfare. Modern scholars generally periodize Roman republican history by internal developments, such as Brunt's (1971) designation of 287–134 BCE as "The Era of Quiescence" or Flower's (2010) demarcation of 300–180 BCE as the "Third Republic."

7 Cf. Aristotle's observation about the comic mask being ridiculous without causing pain (*Poetics* 1449a35–7).

8 On physical abuse of slaves in Plautus, cf. Parker (1989), Saller (1994: 133–53), Stewart (2012: 80–116), Richlin (2017: 90–104).

9 Basic introductions in Hunt (2018, includes Greek slavery) and Joshel (2010); more advanced synthesis in Bradley (1994). With the relative scarcity of literary, archaeological, and epigraphic sources for Plautus' era, most studies of Roman slavery rely on evidence from imperial times.

10 Cf. Bradley (1994: 70): "*rustici* were automatically inferior to *urbani* (at least in a slaveowner's judgement)." His parenthesis accords with New Comedy's urban perspective.

11 Scheidel (2011: 297); cf. Hopkins (1978: 1–37).

12 Burton (2020: 302); Hopkins (1978: 33).

13 Leigh (2004: 88). For manumission and freedmen, cf. Hopkins (1978: 115–32), Mouritsen (2011).

14 We can only guess at population totals and percentages for citizens and slaves, because "even the appropriate order of magnitude remains a matter of intense dispute" (Scheidel 2008: 17; cf. de Ligt 2012). Some guestimates for Plautus' era may be useful: census figures generally hover above 250,000 adult male citizens; adding boys under seventeen, women, and girls would suggest roughly 1.5 million Roman citizens; the slave population might approximate 250,000 persons. The percentage of slaves likely increased in the decades after Plautus.

15 Two books may represent ends of a scholarly spectrum: McCarthy (2000) argues that the comic portrayals of slaves alleviated the burden of mastery felt by the Roman aristocracy that bankrolled the plays (a top-down

approach making Plautus complicit with the elite); Richlin (2017; summary exposition in Richlin [2020]) argues that the plays were composed and performed by, for, and about the slave experience (a bottom-up approach making Plautus a champion of the oppressed). See also Fitzgerald (2019). Whereas those studies are fundamentally literary rather than historical, Stewart (2012; summary exposition in Stewart [2020]) analyzes slavery in Plautus based upon contemporary Roman laws and political history.

16 Though lacking discussion of torture and crucifixion, Beard (2014) usefully defamiliarizes the Roman sense of humor.

17 On the opportunities and limits for an ancient slave to exercise agency, cf. Hunt (2018: 137–54), Stewart (2012: 50–5; 2020).

18 Lydus in *Bacchides* typifies a Plautine strict tutor; Janka (2004: 64) likens Tranio to an Anti-Mentor of *Odyssey*.

19 Cf. Fraenkel (2007: 167) on such Plautine slave monologues as "a kind of catechism of the duties of a good servant."

20 Bradley (1994: 4): "the institution itself has to be approached primarily in terms of the social relationship which bound slave and slaveowner together"; cf. Stewart (2012: 1–13).

21 Fontaine (2010: 226–30) connects comic parasites with pederasty, and the adjective "filthy" (*impurus*, a word of strong moral rebuke) corroborates that connection.

22 Richlin (2017: 126–36).

23 Sonnenschein (1907: 131) equates counterfeiting with stale jokes; Gunderson (2015: 70–2) explores self-definition versus self-deception. Debased or counterfeit coins were a real problem; for example, 25 percent of the Carthaginians' first payment of war indemnity in 199 BCE was found to be alloy rather than pure silver (Livy 32.2.2).

24 Recalcitrant Pinacium, not loyal Phaniscus, may be the attendant that Callidamates smacks upon arrival at the party (314); cf. Sonnenschein (1907: 98).

25 In performance terms, Marshall (2006: 88) observes that "the largest roles in Plautus all require the leading actors to play slaves."

26 Stürner (2020: 137).

27 (2020: 143); cf. Frederick Douglass' remark that "[t]he morality of a *free* society can have no application to *slave* society" (1855: ch. XIV, 191, italics his).

28 James (2020).

29 Witzke (2015: 23 n.6); all six of Terence's plays include sex labor. Marshall (2013) makes important comparisons with sex slavery in contemporary Cambodia.

30 Witzke (2015: 12); cf. Adams (1983). Translating *meretrix* as "prostitute" is perhaps too vague. Slang ages quickly and often carries derogatory overtones. "Courtesan," though a bit old fashioned, is not necessarily a bad translation (*pace* Witzke) for its ability to emphasize a play's exotic Greek setting and *hetaerae* as glamorous embodiments of male fantasy. "Sex laborer" (as Witzke prefers) best fits the role for historical analysis but sounds unwieldy and bureaucratic for staged comedy.

31 Dutsch (2015: 27–9).

32 On Roman content, Williams (1958). Translations mute the scene's coded Roman language for the polarity of *meretrix* and *matrona*; cf. Strong (2016, esp. 28–32).

33 Case studies of freedwomen as concubines in the Roman jurists date from centuries later (McGinn 1991). Glazebrook (2014) compares Philematium's manumission with that of the historical Neaera in Greece. Chrysis in Menander's *Samia* offers a New Comic parallel, although she was the concubine of the absent father rather than the present son; cf. Rosivach (1998: 113–15), Wright (2021: 46–8).

34 Mouritsen (2011: 36–65).

35 Felson's (1997) narratological analysis of Penelope choosing her roles among potential plots of reunion, remarriage, dalliance, or adultery nicely aligns with performance criticism of female characters choosing objectives that are sometimes opaque to other characters.

36 Marshall (2013: 192–4) examines Philematium's "true love" as a rational and moral acquiescence for survival. Vidović (2019: 128) proposes that her "being the only true beloved turns out to be nothing more than a usual customer request, as legitimate as any other male fantasy that the *meretrix* is expected to fulfill." Owens (2001: 223) may go too far in suggesting that Philematium is aware that Philolaches eavesdrops, but as a freed *meretrix* she is an actor always on stage who "feigns for a living, enchanting the spectator" (Duncan 2006: 258).

37 On Roman dowries, Saller (1994: 204–24); in Plautus, Braund (2005: 48–50). There existed two types of marriage in Plautus' era: *cum manu* (in which the wife passed into the authority of the husband's family) and *sine*

manu (in which she remained under her natal family's). Plautus does not clearly distinguish them.

38 Cf. Philippides (1999: 87–8).

39 Polybius 31.25.4. Polybius then records Cato's dismay that pretty boys cost more than fields and fish more than plowmen. How expensive are Tranio's fish dinners?

40 The precise denomination signified by a *nummus* varies in Plautus. At *Mostellaria* 357, when Tranio directly addresses Roman soldiers as men earning three *nummi*, it specifically denotes the Roman bronze *as* (one-tenth of a silver *denarius*), for a legionary's pay at the time was three *asses* per day (Crawford 1974: 632).

41 For basics of the Roman economy and coinage, Harl (1996: 30–45); full treatment of the era's economic transformations in Kay (2014); on economic motives for aggression, Harris (1985: 54–104, overstating the case); for acceleration of luxury in the 180s BCE, de Ligt (2015).

42 On Roman moneylending and banking, see Barlow (1978: esp. 68–76 on *Mostellaria*). On the financial crisis, cf. Livy 35.7.1–5 and 35.41.9, Barlow (1978: 57–60), Feeney (2010: esp. 295). Suggestively for *Mostellaria*, the relief of debtors was slated to take effect on the Feralia, the final day of the Parentalia, a feast of the *Manes* (Livy 35.7.3; cf. King 2020: 152–3 on Feralia).

43 *de Agricultura* 1.1 (the tract's only mention of moneylending). Ever the moralizing politician, Cato likened moneylenders to murderers (Cicero, *de Officiis* 2.89) even as he himself profited from the practice; see Astin (1978: 319–23).

44 See Lewis (1986) for the analogy and representative biographies of Greek immigrants to Egypt.

45 Cf. Slater (2016: 63) on *Mostellaria*'s Athenian setting suggesting "a fantasy Greek housing bubble." Lewis (1986: 20) notes the prevalent moneymaking opportunity in Ptolemaic Egypt whereby middlemen leased allotments from mercenaries and sublet those allotments to native Egyptian farmers. Such activity would be a reasonable conjecture for Theopropides' (or his Greek equivalent's) venture.

46 Nichols (2010: 49). Her study juxtaposes *Mostellaria* and Cato to conclude that "the idea of the house as a potential site of sumptuary vice" (56) already existed in the time of Plautus. Cf. Leach (1969: 324–7) on Simo's house being Greek.

47 Nichols (2010: 56).

48 Roth (2012).

49 Cf. Astin (1978: 240–66), Kay (2014: 147–61).

50 See Gowers (1993: 50–108, esp. 51–66) on foods in Plautus as complex codes for constructing Greek versus Roman and urban versus rural.

51 In Plautus and Livy, the *Macellum* most likely is identical with the fish market known as the Forum Piscarium (Piscatorium); see Richardson (1992: 169).

52 Quotations from Gruen (2014: 603, 607, 609), though he is not unique in chasing after the phantom of Intentional Fallacy and authorial intent (on which, see Wimsatt and Beardsley 1946). We cannot interview Plautus in a scholarly séance.

53 Wallace-Hadrill (1994: 60), studying houses in Pompeii; Milnor (2002) indicates that such an ideology existed in Plautus' era.

54 Wilshire (1990).

55 Amid its guided tour of the Roman Forum, *Curculio* (480–1) alludes to shifty bankers loaning at interest; see Moore (1991: 353–4).

56 Misargyrides must yell "Philolaches" at line 587 ("Now, by Hercules, I'll name him!"). Extant manuscripts have not preserved the naming, but Tranio praises Misragyrides' bellowing (587–8) and Theopropides asks "Why is he dunning my son Philolaches?" (616–17).

57 Before noon proved at line 651; Philolaches greets Tranio's return with fancy provisions (363), but Tranio went to the Piraeus to shop for evening supper (67) rather than luncheon.

58 *Comissatio* at 317, 335, and 989 (by Phaniscus). On Roman festive drinking and dining see Dunbabin (2003, with illustrations); on ideology and practice of men and women reclining together and the *comissatio* see Roller (2006: 98–106; 181–8). On symposia, cf. Lowe (1995: 24–9) for Plautus and Konstantakos (2005) for Greek comedy.

59 Callon (2013).

60 On extravagant dinners and sumptuary laws as economic and political transformations, cf. de Ligt (2015: esp. 379–81), Rosivach (2006); on the laws as "symbolic resistance to Hellenic influence," Gruen (1990: 170–4).

61 Segal (1987: 15–69).

62 Since there were no purpose-built Roman theaters before 55 BCE, theatrical venues can be seen as "theater-temples"; cf. Hanson (1959), Goldberg (1998).

63 Jeppesen (2015).

64 First *lectisternium*: Livy 5.13.5–8; it is impossible to determine if that celebration served as a charter ritual. Livy's remark that *lectisternia* at some temples occurred throughout most of the year (36.1.2; 42.30.8) implies a distinction between regular and extraordinary *lectisternia*.

65 Cf. the funeral *ludi* of the Pontifex Maximus in 183 BCE, which included a public distribution of meat, 120 gladiators fighting, and afterwards a splendid *epulum* with dining tables set up throughout the Forum (Livy 39.46.1–3).

66 Cf. Castellani (1988: 68–9) that *Mostellaria* was staged in the Forum as part of funeral *ludi*. Plautus also sprinkles *ludi/ludere* a dozen times throughout the course of a few other plays (*Amphitruo, Miles Gloriosus, Pseudolus,* and *Casina*).

67 Frangoulidis (2014) fancies the party indoors as a ghost of its outdoor incarnation, Tranio as an Orcus-figure, and Theopropides as dead in his opposition to Greek morality and revived by his eventual acceptance of it. We may wonder who, or what, is the play's titular little *monstrum*?

68 Flower (1996: 106).

69 Cf. Boyle (2006: 3–5); Sumi (2002) on aristocratic and imperial funerals; Johanson (2011) on the spatial and visual elements of funeral processions; Flower (1996: 91–127) is fundamental for the role of ancestor masks in funerals; Bettini (2011: 225–37) is insightful and alert to Plautine resonances.

70 Cf. *Amphitruo*'s prologue, in which Mercury explains that Jupiter converts himself into the *imago* of Amphitryon (*vortit sese imaginem*) because he becomes an actor/skin-changer/werewolf whenever he wishes (*vorsipellem se facit*, 121–3); Bettini (2011: 191–2).

71 King (2020: 1–29).

72 We might compare elements in the various regional rituals of Mexican Día de Muertos celebrations.

73 Dolansky (2011) argues that the Parentalia honored kin in a much broader sense than direct ancestors; cf. King (2020: 149–60).

74 Cf. Dolansky (2019) on Lemuria's concern with the untimely dead related to the domestic space (e.g., infants buried on the premises), King (2020: 160–71) on the Lemuria and Ovid's blurring of *Manes* and *Lemures*.

75 Ogden (2009: 146).

76 Sourcebooks: Ogden (2009) and Hansen (2017: 17–18, 112–28); Crowley (2019) explores the phenomenology of ghosts in Roman visual culture.

77 Texts and brief commentaries in Ogden (2009: 154–61, 316–19). Felton (1999) places the accounts of Pliny and Lucian within oral folkloric

traditions. Lucian's *Philopseudes* (*Lover of Lies*) satirizes superstition through amusing anecdotes. Its first story of haunting (27) pertains little to *Mostellaria*. Its second story (30–1) embellishes Pliny's tale to ridicule it. Felton (1999: 88) posits tenuous connection between *Mostellaria* and Lucian's second story.

78 On modern ghost stories, Grider (2007). Luckily, Rome appears to have been zombie-free.

79 The twelve extant verses of Livius Andronicus' *Aegistus* (Boyle 2006: 30–3) suggest Cassandra's presence, and the line "none of you should rehash these events with the woman" might indicate a response to her seeing ghosts of the slain.

80 Padilla Peralta (2017: 345).

81 Felton (1999: 58–60) observes the flaws and inconsistencies in Tranio's "mangled," "hastily improvised and frantically delivered" tale, including how a ghost that initially appeared in a dream now has physical form to knock the door as a poltergeist, that a murder sixty years ago would make the house's previous owner quite old, and that the vague allusion to apparitions (*monstra*, 505) remains undeveloped.

82 For text, translation, and commentary, Diggle (2004: 111–13, 349–75); for relations to Menander and New Comedy, Pertsinidis (2018: 45–68).

83 Rüpke (2012: 77), who argues, however, that the masked actors in funerals represented statues of ancestors rather than "dead people rumbling through their city."

84 See Flower (1996: 185–222) on *imagines* in the home, especially 202 on *imagines* as spectators of and possibly participants in daily activities, and 217–20 on the daily greeting of clients and patrons.

Chapter 3

1 On "theater without theaters," see Goldberg (2018), whose work with virtual reality imaging offers useful challenges and correctives to long-held views. Note his description of the Forum as "the most physically irregular, socially diverse, unregulated public space in the city, a jumble of houses, shops, temples, and civic structures alive with the concomitant sights, sounds, and smells of commercial, religious, and civic life." (2018: 152).

2 Marshall (2006: 35–48). Since plays were staged in the sight of the honored divinity, drama accompanying the inauguration of temples likely was staged in adjacent open areas; cf. Hanson (1959: 17–18), Goldberg (1998). Plays could share locations with other entertainments at the *ludi*, sometimes contentiously: the prologue to Terence's *Hecyra* (39–42) claims that the play's performance during L. Aemilius Paullus' funeral in 160 BCE was interrupted by a crowd rushing in to secure places for an upcoming gladiatorial show.

3 Manuwald (2011: 64): "From the earliest times the stage was the essential feature of a Roman theatre." Cf. Livy (40.51.3) on a proposal to construct a *theatrum et proscaenium* (= *scaena*), which indicates the centrality of the *scaena* and its separability from the *theatrum/cavea*.

4 Cf. Groton (2020), Wiseman (2015: 50–62).

5 *Bacchides* 831–2 ("Follow me . . . just three single steps." "Or ten.") seems to indicate the approximate distance between two doorways (three single steps equals about two meters) and relative width of stage (ten steps to go over the edge, i.e., "get off the stage / the hell out of here").

6 Marshall (2006: 52–3). Note that at the funeral games of L. Aemilius Paullus, Terence staged both his *Hecyra* (three doors) and *Adelphoe* (two doors).

7 Lowe (1995).

8 The idea that the *angiportus* is perpendicular to the street is mistaken (Marshall 2006: 54–5, 107–8). If *Mostellaria* was staged in the Forum, Tranio's claim to convene a senate meeting in back collapses distinctions between the Athenian setting of the play and the Roman venue.

9 Groton (2020: 54). The wall paintings depicting theatrical settings in luxurious houses of Pompeii date from centuries after Plautus and should not be used as evidence for the decoration of his sets.

10 Cf. a joke in *Menaechmi*'s prologue (72–6) about using the same façade for homes of kings, paupers, doctors, etc. in different plays.

11 Cf. *Miles Gloriosus* (901–2, 915–21, 1139), *Poenulus* (1110).

12 Landrum (2015).

13 Groton (2020: 50–1).

14 Marshall (2006: 53–4).

15 On *bōmolochos* as jackdaw and buffoon, Kidd (2012), Fontaine (2010: 174–83); cf. Fay (1903: 249–60) on Tranio's name and various birds.

16 Cf. Oliver (1993).

17 See Lenski (2013) on incense burners (*thymiateria*) and other objects with slave figures as artistic extensions of using slaves as tools. A comic slave *thymiaterion* may pun upon the phrase *servus callidus/calidus* (clever/hot): "Using this object the master could not only burn his incense, he could also mock his troublesome blowhard of a slave while viewing his sculptural likeness fuming atop a smoking altar." (Lenski 2013: 132).

18 Plautus knew his Euripides (e.g., naming him at *Rudens* 86) and exploited his drama; cf. Slater (2000: 181–202) on *Amphitruo* and *Bacchae.*

19 Cf. Marshall (2006: 126–58), Petrides (2014: 433–40), Wiles (1991); Rudlin (1994: 34) on the primacy of the mask for commedia dell'arte: "the personality of the actor is thus overtaken not by an author's scripted character, but by the persona of the mask to be played."

20 Duckworth (1952: 270).

21 Cf. Julius Pollux's (second century CE) catalogue of forty-four Greek New Comic masks, conveniently listed in Wright (2021: 14–17).

22 The Roman imperial scholar Quintilian claims that the comic father's mask had one eyebrow raised and the other normal, such that he could appear stirred up or calm by showing a different side to the spectators (*Institutes* 11.3.74). Even if not true for masks of Plautus' era, Quintilian's claim reveals a tendency to derive characterization from the mask's physiognomy.

23 Cf. Lowe (1997) on Terence; Franko (2004) on Plautus.

24 Being a trilogy, *Oresteia* offers the broadest introduction to the topic; see Marshall (2003).

25 Cf. Marshall (2006: 96–7).

26 For a troupe of seven, stage management is brisk and likely requires a speaking actor (Tranio?) as a mute attendant helping bring on the couch and banqueting equipment before line 308. At line 294 Philematium, probably seated on a couch and with Philolaches standing, sends Scapha away; at 308 she addresses at least one slave with three commands; Callidamates and Delphium enter at 310, and he dismisses his attendant at 314; by 326 a second couch is available for Callidamates and Delphium. Marshall (2006: 111) suggests that eight performers are required, though only seven individuals are listed; this was likely a mistake [personal communication], but eight may be the most likely troupe size.

27 Cf. Marshall (2006: 58). The manuscripts read *canem capram commixtam* (bitch mixed with nanny goat); de Melo and others emend to *caenum κόπρῳ commixtum* (mud mixed with mierda).

28 Philematium either holds up or wears a dress at line 166; she definitely wears it at 172.

29 Cf. Dutsch (2015: 26–30).

30 The *lex Oppia*, passed in 215 BCE during the war with Hannibal and repealed in 195, prohibited women from wearing more than a half ounce of gold or multicolored clothing. Plautus obliquely refers to the law in other plays: cf. Johnston (1980), Gruen (1990: 143–6).

31 Cf. Philippides (1999: 71–5) on the opening scene as the first of four sieges, the others being: the lockout of Theopropides; Phaniscus and Pinacium; negotiations to enter Simo's house. Milnor (2002) explores the play's (im)permeable boundaries, of outside/inside, public/private, male/female, old/young. Pages 111–14 link Tranio to Hermes, the trickster god of transgressing boundaries.

32 See Mariotti (1992: 105–13). His proposal to read *nidor, et aperi* (stinkpot, and open up!) in line 5 is tempting for its clarity of staging.

33 Marshall (2006: 63–4) unpacks the innuendo: Callidamates will fall to the ground; his erection will fall; the lovers will tumble in bed. Since a prop cannot be introduced without motivation or explanation, *hoc* cannot refer to some random parcel she carries. Heywood's close adaptation in *The English Traveller* boldly grasps the phallic innuendo: *First Wench*: "Stand up stiff . . . If thou fall, I'll fall with thee." *Rioter*: "Now I sink, / And as I dive and drown, thus by degrees / I'll pluck thee to the bottom." (2.2.18–22). Cf. Phaniscus' ambiguous "this" at line 870: perhaps his back, his hand, or his phallus (Richlin 2017: 345).

34 *Truculentus* 373, with a *meretrix* coaxing an extravagant customer, corroborates this staging: "Gimme a kiss?" "How 'bout ten instead!" "Mua [*em*]! That's why you're broke."

35 Cf. Padilla Peralta (2017: 337).

36 Paul Menzer [personal communication].

37 Moore (1998). Longer confidential monologues can serve a structural function of opening and closing major units of action (e.g., Tranio's at 348–62, 408–18 plus 426–30, 536–46, 775–83, and 1041–63).

38 Moore (1998: *passim*, esp. 33–6).

39 Plautus arranges for Tranio to overcome "two at a time" (Stürner 2020: 146), thereby "exaggerating Tranio's danger . . . to enhance his heroic stature" (Lowe 1985: 13). Such gains rebuff (e.g.) de Melo's complaints about the "awkward inactivity" of Misargyrides and Theopropides in Plautus' reshaping of the Greek staging (2011: 310–11).

40 Since Misargyrides exits via the wing beside Simo's house (654), Tranio and Theopropides will face that direction, which can inspire Tranio's hot lie that Simo is the seller (663).

41 Cf. Slater (2000: 140): "Plautine theatre, then, is not mimetic in nature but metatheatric." Other valuable discussions of Plautine metatheater in English include Moore (1998), Batstone (2005), Bungard (2020, a succinct overview).

42 Cf. Slater (2000: 142): "We the audience and Tranio, then, are by implication awake; we are superior to the unfortunate *senes* wrapt in the dream Tranio has spun for them." Sonnenschein (1907: 127) and Fay (1902: 132) apply "they sleep" to the old men, and Fay adds that *arte* puns as snugly / by my artifice.

43 Cf. Marshall (2006: 193–4).

44 Cf. Frangoulidis (1997: 38–50).

45 Cf. Philippides (1999: 106–9) on Callidamates as orator in the finale. On Plautus and oratory, cf. Barbiero (2020), Hanses (2020b: 123–200).

46 Marshall's chapter on improvisation clarifies many misconceptions and provides foundations for further study (2006: 245–79). Cf. Slater (2000: 163–74) on scripted improvisation; Vogt-Spira (2001) on the intersection of scripted Greek and unscripted Italian traditions.

47 Marshall (2006: 253–4) and Bungard (2020: 248 fn.2) adduce jazz as an analogy.

48 Cf. Lowe's analysis (1985: 9–13) of Plautine alterations to the scene's Greek model.

49 Goldberg (2018: 149).

50 Gellar-Goad (2020) offers an accessible introduction to Plautine meter and music through an analysis of *Bacchides*. Gratwick (1993: 40–63) combines rigorous analysis of Plautine meter with practical advice on how to read it, plus debunks many misrepresentations among ancient and early modern authors. Moore (2012) consolidates his decades of research into a comprehensive study. The definitive work on Plautine meter is Questa's (2007).

51 I say pure iamb because Latin versification depends upon metrical quantity rather than stress accent or number of syllables. Latin meter permitted numerous substitutions, such as two short/light syllables for one long/heavy, a practice familiar to those who have studied the dactylic hexameters of Homer or Vergil. Importantly, since very few verses consist solely of pure iambs or pure trochees, the number of syllables in a verse of Plautus varies considerably more than (e.g.) English iambic pentameter.

52 In arguing that all meters outside *ia*[6] were sung, Moore (2012) minimizes the difference in delivery between *cantica* and trochees.

53 Cf. Duckworth (1952: 372), Moore (2012: 196–7). Duckworth proposes that an implicit rising rhythm of the bacchiac-iambic sequences buttresses the theme of construction, and a falling rhythm of the cretic-trochaic sequences suggests collapse.

54 Sonnenschein (1907: 148) adduces Cicero's comment comparing a lawyer changing arguments to a *tibicen* crossing the stage (*pro Murena* 12.26). Granting Moore's (2012: 28–9) objections to using Cicero's remark as evidence for the onstage presence of *tibicines* in the *palliata*, the comparison does suggest plausible choreography for Philolaches-as-orator.

55 Moore (2012: 183).

56 Marshall (2006: 218) suggests that "winding down" is a technique unique to *Mostellaria*.

57 Moore (2012: 185).

58 Gellar-Goad (2020: 255). Tobias (1979) emphasizes the meter's *gravitas* and *dignitas* and use in master–slave encounters.

59 Good remarks on Phaniscus and Pinacium in Moore (2012: 295–300), who observes that after over 500 lines Tranio has finally left the stage and "[a]s soon as the mastermind of the deception has left, that deception begins to crumble, and the metrical orderliness of the music crumbles along with it."

60 Marshall (2006: 207–25).

61 Moore (2012: 251).

62 Moore catalogues the exceptions (2012: 399–402).

63 Marshall (2006: 223) notes a range from six plays with four arcs to one with seven.

64 Sharrock (2009: 97): "Plot makes comedy, but paradoxically plot is funny precisely when it fails to make progress; or, perhaps, we should see comedy as divided into plot and anti-plot, each of which requires the other." Cf. Slater on improvisation (2000: 164): "[t]here were always episodes which

lead nowhere. Such passages, however, were not themselves failures, if the spectators found enjoyment in them."

65 Moore (1998: 41) suggests that the progression leads an audience to sympathize with the revelers, from the moral uprightness of Grumio to the remorse of Philolaches to the affection and gratitude of Philematium to the "fascination and fun" of the party.

66 As Marshall notes from experience (2006: 81). The Roman practice of *instauratio*, repeating a ritual because of real or imagined irregularities, offered religious justification for compelling an encore performance.

67 Moore (1998: 93–101); cf. Philippides' observation that with the actors' reentry onto an empty stage at *Mostellaria* 858 "it seems as if the comedy begins afresh." (1999: 93).

68 Cf. Sharrock (2009: 257–8) for the emphasis on *this* play, though I am less bullish on claims of "comic harmony and mutual reconciliation."

Chapter 4

1 Ferri (2020) provides a sound introduction; cf. Marshall (2006: 274–8) for scripts as transcripts.

2 Current practice for these early modern plays prefers adoption of one version for printing or performing rather than conflating different versions. On *Faustus*, Marcus (1989); on *Lear*, Taylor and Warren (1986), but cf. Foakes (1997) for a thoughtful defense of conflation.

3 Cf. Sonnenschein (1907: 61).

4 Cf. Sonnenschein (1907: 162). On doublets and improvisation, see Marshall (2006: 266–71).

5 Sonnenschein argues for cutting lines 224–44 rather than 208–23 (1907: 150, 152); Leo (1913: 114 n.1) sees lines 208–23 as a substitute for 186–207.

6 See Hanses (2020b) on the afterlife of Roman comedy in oratory, satire, and love poetry.

7 Polt (2021).

8 In the sixteenth century, Italian familiarity with Plautus in performance generally came through vernacular adaptations. The earliest attested public staging of *Mostellaria* was in 1503 in Ferrara. Cf. Guastella (2020), Hardin (2018, with a good timeline of European reception 1428–1600: 22–7).

9 Camerarius also erred in unnecessarily moving one scene; see Sonnenschein (1907: xxi–ii). Textual instability thus plagued *Mostellaria*'s early modern reception. Cf. Ferri (2020: 411–15).
10 Citations of Shakespeare from Greenblatt et al. (2008).
11 Cf. Miola (1994: 62–79).
12 Pollard (2017: 117–42).
13 Cf. Plautus' Chrysalus boasting that he surpasses slaves named Parmeno or Syrus (*Bacchides* 649–50), his Menandrean prototypes or competitors (p. 7).
14 Cf. Franko (2020); Hardin: "[e]arly modern comedy was Plautine" (2018: 14); Duckworth: "[f]rom the beginnings of English comedy to the end of the Elizabethan period the robust humor of Plautus had been preferred to the more sentimental comedies of Terence" (1952: 428).
15 The spotty ephemeral records for performances of classical plays in early modern England document only two or three performances of *Mostellaria* (1559 at Cambridge University, 1569 at Westminster School, and possibly 1586 at Cambridge University). The low number is typical for documented performances of Plautine plays (*Miles Gloriosus* tops the list with only five); cf. the *Archive of Performances of Greek & Roman Drama* (http://www.apgrd.ox.ac.uk/), Smith (1988).
16 Citations of *The English Traveller* from Wiggins (2008).
17 Rowland (2010) explicates the play's blend of ancient comedy and Caroline preoccupations. Rabkin's (1961: 9) brief comparison of Reignald to Face rather than Tranio indicates the limits of isolating simple "influence" amid the complex confluence of multiple theatrical antecedents.
18 On Jonson's appropriations of earlier comedies as "acts of theatrical imperialism," see Watson (1987; quotation on 1, analysis of *The Alchemist* 113–38).
19 *The Alchemist* quoted from Bevington et al. (2002).
20 Cf. Malamud (2001), Cyrino (2005), Candiard (2019: 361–3), Gonçalves (2020: 462–5).
21 On the "eristic impulse" of surpassing the model, Gonçalves (2020: 463). Maurice (2013) on ransacking, interweaving, and metatheater in ancient and postmodern adaptations.
22 Malamud (2001: 203, 206); cf. Cyrino (2005: 170–2).
23 Cf. Nelson (1990: 179–86). Eco's scintillating but thinly argued remarks on the comic, humor, and carnival are relevant: the "[c]omic is always racist: only the others, the Barbarians, are supposed to pay." (1984: 2).

24 Nelson (1990: 93), who contrasts the trickster as "a more settled, less subversive variant of the rogue." Jeremy repeatedly calls Subtle a "rogue," from the play's opening (1.1.4, in reply to "Lick figs / Out at my—") through the lengthy passage quoted above (5.3.71).

25 Moodie (2019) posits connections between Hermes/Mercury and ancient dramatic comedy, including Plautus' *Amphitruo*.

26 Allan (2018) entitles her chapters with compounds of "trans-". For "God of the Hinge," Hyde (1999: 303). Cf. Fay (1903: 249–60) on Tranio and Hermes.

27 Cf. Ellis (1993: 62) on trickster Coyote's "manipulation of liminal phenomena to establish a point of entry into the land of the dead."

28 Hyde (1999: 227).

29 Hyde examines trickster elements in Douglass (1999: 226–51) and concludes that Douglass is no Hermes but rather like Loki, using his liminal status to assail plantation culture (269–71).

30 Lowe (2007: 108).

Editions and English Translations

This companion quotes Plautus in Latin from Wolfgang de Melo's five-volume Loeb edition (2011–13), which offers a good, updated text and a selective critical apparatus. Those seeking fuller reports of variant manuscript readings and proposed emendations will want to consult the Oxford Classical Text of Lindsay (rev. 1910) or Leo (1895–6; the text used in the old Loeb volumes with Nixon's translation, 1924).

The only recent scholarly edition of *Mostellaria* with commentary is in Greek (Mantzilas 2014, with a tremendous bibliography). As for student editions, Sonnenschein's (2nd edn., 1907) provides copious notes on grammar and syntax, with some attention to staging. Fay's (1902) gives many perceptive insights on staging, but some of its commentary goes beyond cringeworthy to outright heinous racism of an earlier Jim Crow era. Sturtevant's (1925) commentary is scanty, and Merrill's (1972) provides a glossary but few notes. Sonnenschein, Fay, and Sturtevant print acute accents above syllables that they believe receive the metrical beat, which can be helpful for reciting aloud.

Among English translations, Erich Segal's (2008; first published 1969) perhaps remains the best available. Segal had a gift for rendering the wit, absurdity, and bounciness of Plautine Latin into an English idiom agreeable to read and fun to perform. Palmer Bovie's translation is smooth to read but less performable (1995; first published 1970). De Melo's Loeb (2011), with facing Latin text, is clear and faithful but not especially stageworthy. Translations in this companion are by the author.

Works Cited

Adams, J. N. (1983), "Words for 'Prostitute' in Latin," *Rheinisches Museum* 126: 321–58.

Allan, A. (2018), *Hermes*, New York: Routledge.

Anderson, W. S. (1993), *Barbarian Play: Plautus' Roman Comedy*, Toronto: University of Toronto Press.

Archive of Performances of Greek & Roman Drama, http://www.apgrd.ox.ac.uk/

Arnott, W. G. (1979–2000), *Menander*, 3 vols, Cambridge, MA: Harvard University Press.

Astin, A. E. (1978), *Cato the Censor*, Oxford: Clarendon Press.

Barlow, C. T. (1978), "Bankers, Moneylenders, and Interest Rates in the Roman Republic," PhD diss., University of North Carolina at Chapel Hill.

Barbiero, E. A. (2016), "'Dissin' the *Dis Exapaton*: Comic One-upmanship in Plautus' *Bacchides*," *Mnemosyne* 69: 648–67.

Barbiero, E. (2020), "*Alii Rhetorica Tongent*: Plautus and Public Speech," in G. F. Franko and D. Dutsch (eds.), *A Companion to Plautus*, 393–406, Hoboken, NJ: John Wiley & Sons.

Barsby, J., ed. and trans. (1986), *Bacchides*, Warminster: Aris & Phillips.

Batstone, W. (2005), "Plautine Farce and Plautine Freedom: An Essay on the Value of Metatheatre," in W. Batstone and G. Tissol (eds.), *Defining Genre and Gender in Latin Literature*, 13–46, New York: Peter Lang.

Beard, M. (2014), *Laughter in Ancient Rome: on Joking, Tickling, and Cracking Up*, Berkeley, CA: University of California Press.

Bettini, M. (2011), *The Ears of Hermes: Communication, Images, and Identity in the Classical World*, trans. W. Short, Columbus, OH: Ohio State University Press.

Bevington, D, Engle, L, Maus, K. E., and Rasmussen, E., eds. (2002), *English Renaissance Drama. A Norton Anthology*, New York: Norton.

Bovie, P., ed. and trans. (1995), *Plautus: The Comedies, Vol. 3*, Baltimore, MD: Johns Hopkins University Press.

Boyle, A. J. (2006), *An Introduction to Roman Tragedy*, New York: Routledge.

Braden, G., Cummings, R., and Gillespie, S., eds. (2011), *The Oxford History of Literary Translation in English: Vol. 2, 1550–1660*, Oxford: Oxford University Press.

Bradley, K. R. (1994), *Slavery and Society at Rome*, New York: Cambridge University Press.

Braund, S. M. (2005), "Marriage, Adultery, and Divorce in Roman Comic Drama," in W. Smith (ed.), *Satiric Advice on Women and Marriage from Plautus to Chaucer*, 39–70, Ann Arbor, MI: University of Michigan Press.

Brunt, P. A. (1971), *Social Conflicts in the Roman Republic*, New York: Norton.

Buck, C. H. (1940), *A Chronology of the Plays of Plautus*, Baltimore, MD: Johns Hopkins University Press.

Bungard, C. (2020), "Metatheater and Improvisation in Plautus," in G. F. Franko and D. Dutsch (eds.), *A Companion to Plautus*, 237–50, Hoboken, NJ: John Wiley & Sons.

Burton P. (2020), "Warfare and Imperialism in and around Plautus," in G. F. Franko and D. Dutsch (eds.), *A Companion to Plautus*, 301–16, Hoboken, NJ: John Wiley & Sons.

Callon, C. (2013), "*Adulescentes* and *Meretrices*: The Correlation between Squandered Patrimony and Prostitutes in the Parable of the Prodigal Son," *The Catholic Biblical Quarterly*, 75: 259–78.

Candiard, C. (2019), "Roman Comedy on Stage and Screen in the Twentieth and Twenty-First Centuries," in M. T. Dinter (ed.), *The Cambridge Companion to Roman Comedy*, 350–66, Cambridge: Cambridge University Press.

Castellani, V. (1988), "Plautus versus *Komoidia*: Popular Farce at Rome," in J. Redmond (ed.), *Farce*, 53–82, Cambridge: Cambridge University Press.

Connors, C. (2004), "Monkey Business: Imitation, Authenticity, and Identity from Pithekoussai to Plautus," *Classical Antiquity*, 23: 179–207.

Conte, G. B. (1994), *Latin Literature: A History*, trans. J. B. Solodow, rev. edn. D. P. Fowler and G. W. Most, Baltimore, MD.: Johns Hopkins University Press.

Crawford, M. H. (1974), *Roman Republican Coinage*, London: Cambridge University Press.

Crowley, P. (2019), *The Phantom Image: Seeing The Dead in Ancient Rome*, Chicago: University of Chicago Press.

Cyrino, M. S. (2005), *Big Screen Rome*, Malden, MA: 2005.

Davidson, J. (1997), *Courtesans and Fishcakes: The Consuming Passions of Classical Athens*, New York: St, Martin's Press.

de Ligt, L. (2012), *Peasants, Citizens and Soldiers: Studies in the Demographic History of Roman Italy 225 BC – AD 100*, Cambridge: Cambridge University Press.

de Ligt, L. (2015), "Production, Trade and Consumption in the Roman Republic," in D. Hammer (ed.), *A Companion to Greek Democracy and the Roman Republic*, 368–85, Malden, MA: John Wiley & Sons.

de Melo, W., ed. and trans. (2011), *Plautus III*, Cambridge, MA: Harvard University Press.

de Melo, W. (2014), "Plautus's Dramatic Predecessors and Contemporaries in Rome," in M. Fontaine and A. C. Scafuro (eds.), *The Oxford Handbook of Greek and Roman Comedy*, 447–61, Oxford: Oxford University Press.

Dickey, S. (1991), "Shakespeare's Mastiff Comedy," *Shakespeare Quarterly* 42: 255–75.

Diggle, J., ed. (2004), *Theophrastus: Characters*, Cambridge: Cambridge University Press.

Dolansky, F. (2011), "Honouring the Family Dead on the *Parentalia*: Ceremony, Spectacle, and Memory," *Phoenix* 65: 125–57.

Dolansky, F. (2019), "Nocturnal Rites to Appease the Untimely Dead: The *Lemuria* in its Socio-Historical Context," *Mouseion* 16: 37–64.

Douglass, F. (1855), *My Bondage and My Freedom*, https://en.wikisource.org/wiki/My_Bondage_and_My_Freedom_(1855)

Duckworth, G. E. (1952), *The Nature of Roman Comedy*, Princeton, NJ: Princeton University Press.

Dunbabin, K. M. (2003), *The Roman Banquet: Images of Conviviality*, Cambridge: Cambridge University Press.

Duncan, A. (2006), *Performance and Identity in the Classical World*, Cambridge: Cambridge University Press.

Dutsch, D. (2015), "Feats of Flesh: The Female Body on the Plautine Stage," in D. Dutsch, S. James, and D. Konstan (eds.), *Women in Roman Republican Drama*, 17–36, Madison, WI: University of Wisconsin Press.

Eco, U. (1984), "The Frames of Comic 'Freedom,'" in T. Sebeok (ed.), *Carnival!*, 1–9, New York: Mouton.

Ellis, L. (1993), "Trickster: Shaman of the Liminal," *Studies in American Indian Literatures*, series 2, vol. 5: 55–68.

Fay, E. W., ed. (1902), *The Mostellaria of Plautus*, Boston: Allyn and Bacon.

Fay, E. W. (1903), "Further Notes on the *Mostellaria* of Plautus," *American Journal of Philology* 24: 245–77.

Feeney, D. (2010), "Crediting Pseudolus: Trust, Belief, and the Credit Crunch in Plautus' *Pseudolus*," *Classical Philology* 105: 281–300.

Feeney, D. C. (2016), *Beyond Greek: The Beginnings of Latin Literature*, Cambridge, MA: Harvard University Press.

Felson, N. (1997), *Regarding Penelope: From Character to Poetics*, Norman, OK: University of Oklahoma Press.

Felton, D. (1999), *Haunted Greece and Rome: Ghost Stories from Classical Antiquity*, Austin, TX: University of Texas Press.

Ferri, R. (2020), "The Textual Tradition of Plautus," in G. F. Franko and D. Dutsch (eds.), *A Companion to Plautus*, 407–18, Hoboken, NJ: John Wiley & Sons.

Fitzgerald, W. (2019), "Slaves and Roman Comedy," in M. T. Dinter (ed.), *The Cambridge Companion to Roman Comedy*, 188–99, Cambridge: Cambridge University Press.

Flower, H. I. (1996), *Ancestor Masks and Aristocratic Power in Roman Culture*, Oxford: Clarendon Press.

Flower, H. I. (2010), *Roman Republics*, Princeton, NJ: Princeton University Press.

Foakes, R. A. (1997), "Shakespeare Editing and Textual Theory: A Rough Guide," *Huntington Library Quarterly* 60: 425–42.

Fontaine, M. (2010), *Funny Words in Plautine Comedy*, Oxford: Oxford University Press.

Fontaine, M. (2014), "Between Two Paradigms: Plautus," in M. Fontaine and A. C. Scafuro (eds.), *The Oxford Handbook of Greek and Roman Comedy*, 516–37, Oxford: Oxford University Press.

Fraenkel, E. (2007), *Plautine Elements in Plautus*, trans. T. Drevikovsky and F. Muecke, New York: Oxford University Press.

Frangoulidis, S. (1997), *Handlung und Nebenhandlung: Theater, Metatheater und Gattungsbewusstsein in der römischen Komödie*, Stuttgart: M&P Verlag.

Frangoulidis, S. (2014), "Renewal and Compromise in Plautus' *Mostellaria*," in I. Persynakis and E. Karakasis (eds.), *Plautine Trends: Studies in Plautine Comedy and Its Reception*, 127–39, Berlin: de Gruyter.

Franko, G. F. (2004), "Ensemble Scenes in Plautus," *American Journal of Philology* 125: 27–59.

Franko, G. F. (2020), "Plautus in Early Modern England," in G. F. Franko and D. Dutsch (eds.), *A Companion to Plautus*, 445–59, Hoboken, NJ: John Wiley & Sons.

Gellar-Goad, T. H. M. (2020), "Music and Meter in Plautus," in G. F. Franko and D. Dutsch (eds.), *A Companion to Plautus*, 251–67, Hoboken, NJ: John Wiley & Sons.

Gellar-Goad, T. H. M. (2021), *Plautus: Curculio*, New York: Bloomsbury Academic.

Germany, R. (2019), "The Politics of Roman Comedy," in M. T. Dinter (ed.), *The Cambridge Companion to Roman Comedy*, 66–84, Cambridge: Cambridge University Press.

Glazebrook, A. (2014), "The Erotics of Manumission: Prostitutes and the πρᾶσις ἐπ' ἐλευθερίᾳ," *EuGeStA* 4: 53–80.

Goldberg, S. M. (1990), "Act to Action in Plautus' *Bacchides*," *Classical Philology* 85: 191–201.

Goldberg, S. M. (1998), "Plautus on the Palatine," *Journal of Roman Studies* 88: 1–20.

Goldberg, S. M. (2018), "Theater without Theaters: Seeing Plays the Roman Way," *TAPA* 148: 139–72.

Goldberg, S. M. (2019), *Terence: Andria*, New York: Bloomsbury Academic.

Gonçalves, R. T. (2020), "Reception Today: Theater and Movies," in G. F. Franko and D. Dutsch (eds.), *A Companion to Plautus*, 461–71, Hoboken, NJ: John Wiley & Sons.

Gowers, E. (1993), *The Loaded Table: Representations of Food in Roman Literature*, Oxford: Clarendon Press.

Gratwick A. S. (1982), "Drama," in E. J. Kenney and W. V. Clausen (eds.), *Cambridge History of Latin Literature*, Vol 2., 77–137, Cambridge: Cambridge University Press.

Gratwick, A. S., ed. (1993), *Plautus: Menaechmi*, Cambridge: Cambridge University Press.

Greenblatt, S., Cohen, W., Howard, J. and Maus, K., eds. (2008), *The Norton Shakespeare*, 2nd edn., New York: Norton.

Grider, S. A. (2007), "Haunted Houses," in D. Goldstein, S. Grider, and J. Thomas (eds.), *Haunting Experiences: Ghosts in Contemporary Folklore*, 143–70, Logan, UT: Utah State University Press.

Groton, A. H. (2020), "Stages and Stagecraft," in G. F. Franko and D. Dutsch (eds.), *A Companion to Plautus*, 47–60, Hoboken, NJ: John Wiley & Sons.

Gruen, E. S. (1990), *Studies in Greek Culture and Roman Policy*, Berkeley, CA: University of California Press.

Gruen, E. S. (1992), *Culture and National Identity in Republican Rome*, Ithaca, NY: Cornell University Press.

Gruen, E. S. (2014), "Roman Comedy and the Social Scene," in M. Fontaine and A. C. Scafuro (eds.), *The Oxford Handbook of Greek and Roman Comedy*, 601–14, New York: Oxford University Press.

Guastella, G. (2020), "From Ferrara to Venice: Plautus in Vernacular and Early Italian Comedy (1486–1530)," in G. F. Franko and D. Dutsch (eds.), *A Companion to Plautus*, 429–43, Hoboken, NJ: John Wiley & Sons.

Gunderson, E. (2015), *Laughing Awry: Plautus and Tragicomedy*, Oxford: Oxford University Press.

Handley, E. W. (1968), *Menander and Plautus: A Study in Comparison*, London: University College.

Hansen, W. (2017), *The Book of Greek and Roman Folktales, Legends, and Myths*, Princeton, NJ: Princeton University Press.

Hanses, M. (2020a), "Men among Monuments: Roman Topography and Roman Memory in Plautus' *Curculio*," *Classical Philology* 115: 630–58.

Hanses, M. (2020b), *The Life of Comedy after the Death of Plautus and Terence*, Ann Arbor, MI: University of Michigan Press.

Hanson, J. A. (1959), *Roman Theater-Temples*, Princeton, NJ: Princeton University Press.

Hardin, R. F. (2018), *Plautus and the English Renaissance of Comedy*, Madison, NJ: Fairleigh Dickinson Press.

Harl, K. W. (1996), *Coinage in the Roman Economy 300 B.C. to A.D. 700*, Baltimore, MD: Johns Hopkins University Press.

Harris, W. V. (1985), *War and Imperialism in Republican Rome, 327–70 B.C.*, rpt. with corrections, Oxford: Oxford University Press.

Hopkins, K. (1978), *Conquerors and Slaves*, Cambridge: Cambridge University Press.

Hunt, P. (2018), *Ancient Greek and Roman Slavery*, Hoboken, NJ: John Wiley & Sons.

Hyde, L. (1999), *Trickster Makes This World: Mischief, Myth, and Art*, New York: North Point Press.

James, S. J. (2020), "Plautus and the Marriage Plot," in G. F. Franko and D. Dutsch (eds.), *A Companion to Plautus*, 109–121, Hoboken, NJ: John Wiley & Sons.

Janka, M. (2004), "Jenseits der Plautus-Analyse: die *Mostellaria* (Gespensterkomödie) als komisch verkehrte Odyssee," in M. Janka (ed.) *Enkyklion Kēpion = Rundgärtchen: zu Poesie, Historie und Fachliteratur der Antike*, 55–80, Munich: Saur.

Jeppesen, S. (2015), "Dictating Parody in Plautus' *Rudens*," *Didaskalia* 12.12, https://www.didaskalia.net/issues/12/12/

Johanson, C. (2011), "A Walk with the Dead: A Funerary Cityscape in Ancient Rome," in B. Rawson (ed.), *A Companion to Families in the Greek and Roman Worlds*, 408–30, Malden, MA: Wiley-Blackwell.

Johnston, P. A. (1980), "*Poenulus* I, 2 and Roman Women," *Transactions of the American Philological Association* 110: 143–59.

Joshel, S. R. (2010), *Slavery in the Roman World*, New York: Cambridge University Press.

Kay, P. (2014), *Rome's Economic Revolution*, Oxford: Oxford University Press.

Kidd, S. (2012), "The Meaning of *Bōmolokhos* in Classical Attic," *Transactions of the American Philological Association* 142: 239–55.

King, C. (2020), *The Ancient Roman Afterlife: Di Manes, Belief, and the Cult of the Dead*, Austin, TX: University of Texas Press.

Konstantakos, I. (2005), "The Drinking Theatre: Staged Symposia in Greek Comedy," *Mnemosyne* 58: 183–217.

Landrum, L. (2015), "*Modus Operandi* of an *Architectus Doli*," in L. Landrum, M. Neveu, and N. Djavaherian (eds.), *Architecture's Appeal*, 218–27, New York: Routledge.

Leach, E. W. (1969), "*De exemplo meo ipse aedificato*: An Organizing Idea in the *Mostellaria*," *Hermes* 97: 318–32.

Leigh, M. (2004), *Comedy and the Rise of Rome*, Oxford: Oxford University Press.

Lenski, N. (2013), "Working Models: Functional Art and Roman Conceptions of Slavery," in M. George (ed.), *Roman Slavery and Roman Material Culture*, 129–57, Toronto: University of Toronto Press.

Leo, F., ed. (1895–6), *Plauti Comoediae*, Berlin: Weidmann.

Leo, F. (1913), *Geschichte der römischen Literatur I*, Berlin: Weidmann.

Lewis, N. (1986), *Greeks in Ptolemaic Egypt*, Oxford: Clarendon Press.

Lindsay, W. M., ed. (1910), *T. Macci Plavti Comoediae*, rev. edn., Oxford: Clarendon Press.

López López , M. (1991), *Los Personajes de la comedia Plautina: nombre y función*, Lleida: Pagès editors.

Lowe, J. C. B. (1985), "Plautine Innovations in the *Mostellaria*," *Phoenix* 39: 6–26.

Lowe, J. C. B. (1995), "Indoor Scenes in Plautus," in L. Benz, E. Stärk, and G. Vogt-Spira (eds.), *Plautus und die Tradition des Stegreifspiels*, 23–31, Tübingen: Gunter Narr.

Lowe, J. C. B. (1997), "Terence's Four-Speaker Scenes," *Phoenix* 51: 152–69.

Lowe, N. J. (2007), *Comedy*, Cambridge: Cambridge University Press.

McCarthy, K. (2000), *Slaves, Masters, and the Art of Authority in Plautine Comedy*, Princeton, NJ: Princeton University Press.

McElduff, S. (2013), *Roman Theories of Translation: Surpassing the Source*, New York: Routledge.

McGinn, T. A. J. (1991), "Concubinage and the *Lex Iulia* on Adultery," *Transactions of the American Philological Association* 121: 335–75.

Malamud, M. (2001), "Brooklyn on the Tiber: Roman Comedy on Broadway and in Film," in S. Joshel, M. Malamud, and D. McGuire (eds.), *Imperial*

Projections: Ancient Rome in Modern Popular Culture, 191–208, Baltimore, MD: Johns Hopkins University Press.

Mantzilas, D., ed. (2014), *Titou Makkiou Plautou: To "Stoicheiōmeno" Spiti (Mostellaria)*, Ioannina: Carpe Diem.

Manuwald, G. (2011), *Roman Republican Theatre*, Cambridge: Cambridge University Press.

Marcus, L. S. (1989), "Textual Indeterminacy and Ideological Difference: The Case of *Doctor Faustus*," *Renaissance Drama*, 20: 1–29.

Mariotti, I. (1992), "La prima scena della *Mostellaria* di Plauto," *Museum Helveticum* 49: 105–23.

Marshall, C. W. (2003), "Casting the *Oresteia*," *Classical Journal* 98: 257–74.

Marshall, C. W. (2006), *The Stagecraft and Performance of Roman Comedy*, Cambridge: Cambridge University Press.

Marshall, C. W. (2013), "Sex slaves in New Comedy," in B. Akrigg and R. Tordoff (eds.), *Slaves and Slavery in Ancient Greek Comic Drama*, 173–96, Cambridge: Cambridge University Press.

Maurice, L. (2013), "*Contaminatio* and Adaptation: The Modern Reception of Ancient Drama as an Aid to Understanding Roman Comedy," *Bulletin of the Institute of Classical Studies* Supplement 126: 445–65.

Merrill, F., ed. (1972), *Plautus: Mostellaria*, New York: Macmillan.

Milnor, K. (2002), "Playing House: Stage, Space, and Domesticity in Plautus's *Mostellaria*," *Helios* 29: 3–25.

Miola, R. S. (1994), *Shakespeare and Classical Comedy*, Oxford: Oxford University Press.

Moodie, E. (2019), "Hermes/Mercury: God of Comedy?," in J. Miller and J. S. Clay (eds.), *Tracking Hermes, Pursuing Mercury*, 107–18, Oxford: Oxford University Press.

Moore, T. J. (1991), "*Palliata Togata*: Plautus, *Curculio* 462–86," *American Journal of Philology* 112: 343–362.

Moore, T. J. (1998), *The Theater of Plautus: Playing to the Audience*, Austin, TX: University of Texas Press.

Moore, T. J. (2012), *Music in Roman Comedy*, Cambridge: Cambridge University Press.

Moore, T. J. (2020), "The State of Roman Theater *c.* 200 BCE," in G. F. Franko and D. Dutsch (eds.), *A Companion to Plautus*, 17–29, Hoboken, NJ: John Wiley & Sons.

Mouritsen, H. (2011), *The Freedman in the Roman World*, Cambridge: Cambridge University Press.

Nelson, T. G. A. (1990), *Comedy: The Theory of Comedy in Literature, Drama, and Cinema*, Oxford: Oxford University Press.

Nichols, M. (2010), "Contemporary Perspectives on Luxury Building in Second-century BC Rome," *Papers of the British School at Rome* 78: 39–61.

Nixon, P., trans. (1924), *Plautus III*, Cambridge, MA: Harvard University Press.

Ogden, D. (2009), *Magic, Witchcraft, and Ghosts in the Greek and Roman Worlds*, 2nd edn., New York: Oxford University Press.

Oliver, A. (1993), "An Incense Burner in the Form of an Actor as a Slave on an Altar," in J. Arce and F. Burkhalter (eds.), *Bronces y religión romana: actas del XI Congreso Internacional de Bronces Antiguos, Madrid, Mayo-Junio, 1990*, 331–6, Madrid: Consejo Superior de Investigaciones Científicas.

Olson, S. D. (2007), *Broken Laughter: Select Fragments of Greek Comedy*, Oxford: Oxford University Press.

Owens, W. (2001), "Plautus' Satire of Roman Ideals in *Rudens, Amphitruo*, and *Mostellaria*," in E. Tylawsky and C. Weiss (eds.), *Essays in Honor of Gordon Williams*, 213–27, New Haven, CT: Yale University Press.

Padilla Peralta, D. (2017), "Slave Religiosity in the Middle Republic," *Classical Antiquity* 36: 317–69.

Panayotakis, C. (2019), "Native Italian Drama and Its Influence on Plautus," in M. T. Dinter (ed.), *The Cambridge Companion to Roman Comedy*, 32–46, Cambridge: Cambridge University Press.

Papaioannou, S. (2016), "Plautus Undoing Himself – What is Funny and What is Plautine in *Stichus* and *Trinummus*," in S. Frangoulidis, S. J. Harrison, and G. Manuwald (eds.), *Roman Drama and Its Contexts*, 167–201, Berlin: de Gruyter.

Papaioannou, S. (2020), "Plautus and the Topography of his World," in G. F. Franko and D. Dutsch (eds.), *A Companion to Plautus*, 287–300, Hoboken, NJ: John Wiley & Sons.

Parker, H. (1989), "Crucially Funny or Tranio on the Couch: The *Servus Callidus* and Jokes about Torture," *Transactions of the American Philological Association* 119: 233–246.

Pertsinidis, S. (2018), *Theophrastus' Characters: A New Introduction*, New York: Routledge.

Petrides, A. (2014), "Plautus between Greek Comedy and Atellan Farce: Assessments and Reassessments," in M. Fontaine and A. C. Scafuro (eds.), *The Oxford Handbook of Greek and Roman Comedy*, 424–43, Oxford: Oxford University Press.

Philippides, K. (1999), "Contrasting houses, contrasting values: an interpretation of Plautus' *Mostellaria* based on mirror scenes," in B. Zimmermann (ed.), *Griechische-römische Komödie und Tragödie III*, 67–112, Stuttgart: Metzler.

Pollard, T. (2017), *Greek Tragic Women on Shakespearean Stages*, Oxford: Oxford University Press.

Polt, C. (2021), *Catullus and Roman Comedy: Theatricality and Personal Drama in the Late Republic*, Cambridge: Cambridge University Press.

Questa, C. (2007), *La metrica di Plauto e di Terenzio*, Urbino: QuatroVenti.

Rabkin, N. (1961), "Dramatic Deception in Heywood's *The English Traveller*," *Studies in English Literature, 1500–1900* 1, no. 2: 1–16.

Richardson, jr., L. (1992), *A New Topographical Dictionary of Ancient Rome*, Baltimore, MD: Johns Hopkins University Press.

Richlin, A. (2017), *Slave Theater in the Roman Republic: Plautus and Popular Comedy*. Cambridge: Cambridge University Press.

Richlin, A. (2020), "Owners and Slaves in and around Plautus," in G. F. Franko and D. Dutsch (eds.), *A Companion to Plautus*, 347–59, Hoboken, NJ: John Wiley & Sons.

Roller, M. B. (2006), *Dining Posture in Ancient Rome: Bodies, Values, and Status*, Princeton, NJ: Princeton University Press.

Rosivach, V. J. (1998): *When a Young Man Falls in Love: The Sexual Exploitation of Women in New Comedy*, New York: Routledge.

Rosivach, V. J. (2006), "The *Lex Fannia Sumptuaria* of 161 BC," *Classical Journal* 102: 1–15.

Roth, U. (2012), "Comic Shackles," *Mnemosyne* 65: 746–9.

Rowland, R. (2010), *Thomas Heywood's Theatre, 1599–1639: Locations, Translations, and Conflict*, Burlington, VT: Ashgate.

Rudlin, J. (1994), *Commedia dell'Arte: An Actor's Handbook*, New York: Routledge.

Rüpke, J. (2012), *Religion in Republican Rome: Rationalization and Ritual Change*, Philadelphia, PA: University of Pennsylvania Press.

Saller, R. P. (1994), *Patriarchy, Property and Death in the Roman Family*, Cambridge: Cambridge University Press.

Scafuro, A. C. (2014), "Comedy in the Late Fourth and Early Third Centuries BCE," in M. Fontaine and A. C. Scafuro (eds.), *The Oxford Handbook of Greek and Roman Comedy*, 199–217, Oxford: Oxford University Press.

Schironi, F. (2013), "The Trickster Onstage: The Cunning Slave from Plautus to *Commedia dell'Arte*," in S. D. Olson (ed.), *Ancient Comedy and Reception*, 447–78, Boston: de Gruyter, 2013.

Scheidel, W. (2008), "Roman Population Size: The Logic of the Debate," in L. de Ligt and S. Northwood (eds.), *People, Land, and Politics: Demographic Developments and the Transformation of Roman Italy 300 BC–AD 14*, 17–70, Boston, MA: Brill.

Scheidel, W. (2011), "The Roman Slave Supply" in K. Bradley and P. Cartledge, *The Cambridge World History of Slavery*, Vol. 1, 287–310, Cambridge: Cambridge University Press.

Segal, E. (1987), *Roman Laughter: The Comedy of Plautus*. 2nd edn., Oxford: Oxford University Press.

Segal, E. (2008), *Plautus: Four Comedies*, New York: Oxford University Press.

Sharrock, A. (2009), *Reading Roman Comedy: Poetics and Playfulness in Plautus and Terence*, Cambridge: Cambridge University Press.

Slater, N. W. (2000), *Plautus in Performance: The Theatre of the Mind*, 2nd edn., Amsterdam: Harwood.

Slater, N. W. (2016), "Speculating in Unreal Estate: Locution, Locution, Locution," in S. Frangoulidis, S. Harrison, and G. Manuwald (eds.), *Roman Drama and Its Contexts*, 43–65, Berlin: de Gruyter.

Smith, B. R. (1988), *Ancient Scripts & Modern Experience on the English Stage 1500–1700*, Princeton, NJ: Princeton University Press.

Sommerstein, A. H., ed. (2014), *Menander in Contexts*, New York: Routledge.

Sonnenschein, E. A., ed. (1907), *T. Macci Plavti Mostellaria*, 2nd edn., Oxford: Clarendon Press.

Stärk, E. (1991), "*Mostellaria* oder *Turbare* statt *sedare*," in E. Lefèvre, E. Stärk, and G. Vogt-Spira (eds.), *Plautus Barbarus: Sechs Kapitel zur Originalität de Plautus*, 107–40, Tübingen: Gunter Narr.

Stewart, R. (2012), *Plautus and Roman Slavery*, Malden, MA: Wiley-Blackwell.

Stewart, R. (2020), "Slave Labor in Plautus," in G. F. Franko and D. Dutsch (eds.), *A Companion to Plautus*, 361–77, Hoboken, NJ: John Wiley & Sons.

Strong, A. K. (2016), *Prostitutes and Matrons in the Roman World*, Cambridge: Cambridge University Press.

Stürner, F. (2020), "The *Servus Callidus* in Charge: Plays of Deception," in G. F. Franko and D. Dutsch (eds.), *A Companion to Plautus*, 135–49, Hoboken, NJ: John Wiley & Sons.

Sturtevant, E. H., ed. (1925), *T. Macci Plavti: Mostellaria*, New Haven, CT: Yale University Press.

Sumi, G. S. (2002), "Impersonating the Dead: Mimes at Roman Funerals," *American Journal of Philology* 123: 559–85.

Taylor, G. and Warren, M., eds. (1986), *The Division of the Kingdoms: Shakespeare's Two Versions of "King Lear,"* Oxford: Clarendon Press.

Telò, M. (2019), "Roman Comedy and the Poetics of Adaptation," in M. T. Dinter (ed.), *The Cambridge Companion to Roman Comedy*, 47–65, Cambridge: Cambridge University Press.

Tobias, A. J. (1979), "Bacchiac Women and Iambic Slaves in Plautus," *Classical World* 73: 9–18.

Vidović, G. (2019), "What (Wo)Men want" in L. Radenović, D. Dimitrijević, and I. Akkad (eds.) *Pathe: The Language and Philosophy of Emotions*, 119–44, Belgrade: University Library.

Vogt-Spira, G. (2001), "Traditions of Theatrical Improvisation in Plautus: Some Considerations," in *Oxford Readings in Menander, Plautus, and Terence*, E. Segal (ed.), 95–106, Oxford: Oxford University Press.

Wallace-Hadrill, A. (1994), *Houses and Society in Pompeii and Herculaneum*, Princeton, N.J.: Princeton University Press.

Watson, R. N. (1987), *Ben Jonson's Parodic Strategy: Literary Imperialism in the Comedies*, Cambridge, MA: Harvard University Press.

Wiggins, M., ed. (2008), *A Woman Killed with Kindness and Other Domestic Plays*, Oxford: Oxford University Press.

Wiles, D. (1991), *The Masks of Menander: Sign and Meaning in Greek and Roman Performance*, Cambridge: Cambridge University Press.

Williams, G. (1958), "Some Aspects of Roman Marriage Ceremonies and Ideals 1," *Journal of Roman Studies* 48: 16–29.

Wilshire, B. (1990), "The Concept of the Paratheatrical," *TDR* 34: 169–78.

Wimsatt, jr., W. K. and Beardsley, M. C. (1946), "The Intentional Fallacy," *The Sewanee Review* 54: 468–88.

Wiseman, T. P. (2015), *The Roman Audience: Classical Literature as Social History*, Oxford: Oxford University Press.

Witzke, S. S. (2015), "Harlots, Tarts, and Hussies?: A Problem of Terminology for Sex Labor in Roman Comedy," *Helios* 42: 7–27.

Wright, J. (1974), *Dancing in Chains: The Stylistic Unity of the Comoedia Palliata*, Rome: American Academy.

Wright, M. (2021), *Menander: Samia*, New York: Bloomsbury Academic.

Index

Readers should also consult the Synopsis (pp. xiv-xv) as an index for discussion of scenes in *Mostellaria*.
* denotes characters in *Mostellaria*

actors 15, 54, 60–4, 79, 81, 93–4
  characters and 7, 38–9, 40, 70, 78
  in funerals 45–7
  male 28, 65, 80
  mute 63–4
  number in *Mostellaria* 61–4, 100, 117–18
  see also stage directions
Aemilius Paullus, L. 46, 125 n.1
Alchemist, The, *see* Jonson, Ben
altar 57–8, 112
amica 28–9, 31
angiportus 56
architecture 15–16, 56–7
arcs xiv–xv, 89–90
Aristotle 8, 90
Aristophanes 5, 18, 103
asides 68, 70–6, 77, 80
Atellan Farce 10, 59
audience17, 21–2, 68, 79, 92
  male 28, 31, 32, 65
  see also asides; *cavea*; hierarchy of rapport

banking, *see* moneylending
bōmolochos xiii, 57

Caecilius Statius 8–9, 10
*Callidamates 24–5, 41, 58–9, 60, 67–8, 69, 92
Camerarius (Joachim Kammermeister) 97
cantica, *see under* meter
Cato the Elder, M. Porcius 35, 37, 39, 42
Catullus 3, 96–7
cavea 54, 70–1, 73–4, 77
character
  actor and 7, 38–9, 40, 70, 78
  meter and 84–6
  stock 59–60, 66, 80, 107
  Theophrastus 51
  see also masks; metatheater
Cicero 7–8, 79
city 23, 37–9
clientage, *see* patrons and clients
coinage 25, 33–4
comedy
  Greek New 3–10, 59, 61, 89, 91, 106
  New 27, 103, 108
  Old 5, 67
  Roman New (*palliata*) 6–10, 26, 58, 59, 61, 64, 89, 98–100, 106, 107–8
  romantic 12, 27
commedia dell'arte 10, 66, 81
costume 64–5, 80
country 12, 20, 23, 37–9
Coyote 111, 113, 114
crow xiii, 16, 56, 70
crucifixion 20, 22, 72, 78
cue lines 66–8, 81

*Delphium 5, 28, 67–8
deus ex machina 58–9, 77
dining 23, 33, 37–8, 41–4
Diphilus 4–6, 15, 16, 77, 91
Donatus, Aelius 26
doors 16, 55–6, 67, 77
  see also liminality

Douglass, Frederick 111, 114, 127 n.27
drinking 38, 41–4, 63–4, 67–8, 88
dunning 41

eavesdropping 30–1, 55, 70–6, 77, 98
Egypt 35–6, 45
English Traveller, The, *see* Heywood, Thomas
Ennius 9, 14, 39
epula 44
Euripides 58–9

fabula 73, 78, 92
farce 8, 10, 86, 90–2, 99
fathers and sons 6–7, 12, 36, 60, 62–3, 100–1
Forum (Roman) 18, 38, 40–1, 45–7, 54, 55, 70, 79
freedmen, freedwomen 21, 26, 28, 29–30
frustrationes (delays/deceptions) 91
funerals 44–7, 52
Funny Thing Happened on the Way to the Forum, A 106–10

garlic 37–8
Gellius, Aulus 7–8, 9, 10, 83
ghosts 11, 16, 45, 47–52, 112, 115–16
*Grumio 12, 19–20, 22–3, 37–9, 65, 67, 109
  in *The Taming of the Shrew* 98–9

Hecuba 99
Hermes xiii, 75, 111–12, 114
  see also Mercury
Heywood, Thomas 98, 106
  English Traveller, The 100–2, 105, 109, 113, 135 n.33
hierarchy of rapport 71–6, 87
Homer 11–15, 82
houses
  haunted x–xi, 48–50, 101, 103, 104–5, 107, 115–16
  Odysseus' 11–13
  onstage 55–7
  in Philolaches' allegory 71, 85, 87
  purchase of 32, 36–7
  Roman 40, 46, 48, 52
  Simo's 15–16, 36, 56, 112
  Theopropides' 36, 67
  see also doors; liminality
Hyde, Lewis 111–13

imago (pl. *imagines*) 47, 48, 52, 115
improvisation 80–2, 91, 114
incense burner 58
Intentional Fallacy 39

Jonson, Ben 98
  Alchemist, The 102–6, 108–9, 111

Lambinus (Denis Lambin) 97–8
lazzi 66, 81, 82
lectisternia 44
Lemuria 48
liminality 71, 112–14
Livius Andronicus 1, 7, 8–9, 13–15
Livy 34, 44
Lucian 49
ludere 45
ludi 18, 43–7, 54–5, 73, 83, 95
  funebres 44–7, 82

Macrobius 42–3
male gaze 31, 32, 40, 65, 96
Manes 47–9, 116
manumission 21, 23
  see also freedmen, freedwomen
manuscripts, *see under* scripts
marriage 12–13, 27, 29, 32, 92, 105, 110
masks 19, 45–7, 52, 59–61, 63, 68
matrona 29–30
  see also uxor dotata
Menander 4–8, 12–13, 51, 84
  Dis Exapaton 6–7
Mercury 47

meretrix 28–9, 80, 107
see also sex laborer
metatheater 65, 76–80, 98, 106
meter xiv–xv, 6, 14, 81–2, 83–90, 119
bacchiac 84, 85, 87–8
cantica 61, 84, 89
changes in 72, 75, 86, 87, 89–90
cretic 84, 85, 86
iambic 83, 84, 86, 87, 89
monody 24, 70, 72, 79, 85
structure 89–90
tone 86–8
trochaic 83–4, 89
mime 10, 45
*Misargyrides 35, 41, 74, 82
moneylending 35, 41
monody, *see under* meter
monologue 70–6, 77, 81
soliloquy 7, 70, 72, 75
morality 12, 26–7, 32–3, 37, 60, 65, 97, 103, 109–10
see also prodigality; sumptuary laws
morigera 29
mos maiorum 39
Mostellaria
America and 110, 114
Athenian setting 17, 18, 36, 38
date 18
ending 13, 58–9, 90–2, 112–14
name x, 5
venue of premiere 17–18 (*see also* Forum)
music 6, 61, 81, 106
see also meter

Naevius 8–9, 83
naturalism 6, 8, 43, 55, 70–1, 74, 76–7, 84

Odysseus 11–15, 31, 57
oratory 3, 43, 79
Oresteia 49, 62
Ovid 48

palliata, *see under* comedy
paratheater 39–52
Parentalia 48, 129 n.42
patrons and clients 30, 44, 52, 72
Penelope 12, 31
pergraecari 38–9
*Phaniscus 24–5, 62
*Philematium 5, 12–13, 28–31, 60, 65, 69, 79–80, 87, 96–7
Philemon 4–6, 15, 16, 51, 91
*Philolaches 12, 60, 62–3, 72, 79, 80, 85–6
and Philematium 29–31, 69, 96–7
*Pinacium 24–5
Plautus, Titus Maccius 1, 83
archaisms 3, 97
and early modern England 97–8
and Greek New Comedy 3–10, 11, 15–16, 77, 91
and Homer's *Odyssey* 11–15
other plays by 78, 107
Amphitruo 47
Bacchides 6–7, 15, 61
Curculio 18, 26
Mercator 78
Poenulus 38
Pseudolus 15, 91–2, 107
Trinummus 4, 44
Pliny the Younger 49–50, 52, 115–16
Polybius 46, 51–2
pornography 108
potions 108–9
prodigality 33, 42–3, 60, 91, 97, 100–1
props 63–6
mirror 29, 65–6, 80

role-doubling 61–3, 117–18

scaena 53–5, 57, 70–1, 83
*Scapha 29–31, 65, 80, 85, 87, 95–6, 101
Scipio Aemilianus 32–3

scortum 28–9, 32, 96
  see also sex laborer
scripts 7–8, 39, 80–1, 93–6, 97, 105
set 55–6
sex 25, 27, 32, 63, 67–8, 108
sex laborer 13, 27–9, 32–3, 36–7, 80, 107
  terms for (*meretrix, amica, scortum*) 28–9
Shakespeare, William 12–13, 61, 98–100, 106
  Comedy of Errors, The 99, 108, 111
  Hamlet 94, 99–100
  Taming of the Shrew, The 98–100, 110
*Simo 32, 45, 62, 69, 75, 79, 86
slaves and slavery 17, 19–27, 27–8, 37, 50, 87–8
  "good" and "bad" 22–5, 26
  peculium 21
  servus callidus 7, 15, 26–7, 30, 56–7, 72–3, 80, 111, 134 n.17
  servus currens 78
  sources of 21
  violence against 19–20, 22, 27, 58, 64, 67
soliloquy, *see under* monologue
*Sphaerio 62, 96
stage
  English 98, 100, 102, 105
  Roman 6, 40, 53–6; *see also* *scaena*
stage directions 66–70
sumptuary laws 43, 65
superstition 50–2, 58
surveillance 22, 31, 39–40, 43, 52, 95, 96
  see also male gaze

Terence 25, 26, 59, 84, 99–100, 108, 123 n.9, 124 n.10, 125 n.1
theater spaces, *see* venues
Theophrastus 51, 60
*Theopropides x–xi, 12, 16, 92, 105
  actor 62–3
  bacchiac meter 87–8
  funeral of 45, 47, 112
  in hierarchy of rapport 69, 73–4, 77
  landowner 37
  merchant 35–6, 50, 64
  name 95
  superstitious 50–1, 58
  threatens Tranio 20, 58, 64
tibia 6, 28, 83, 84
tibicen 28, 61, 81, 88, 137 n.54
*Tranio 1, 15–16, 22–3
  in *The Alchemist* [= Jeremy] 102–6, 109
  in *The English Traveller* [= Reignald] 100–2, 113
  ghost story x–xi, 50–1
  and Grumio 19–20, 37–8, 67
  in hierarchy of rapport 72–6
  as magician 66, 112
  metatheater and 77–9
  name xiii
  and Simo 86
  in *The Taming of the Shrew* 98–100
  and Theopropides 24, 57, 87–8, 92
  as trickster 13, 26–7, 45, 57, 82, 111–14
translation and adaptation 4, 11
  English, of *Mostellaria* 97–106, 141
  Roman 1, 3
    of Greek New Comedy 3–10, 15
    of Homer 11–15
tricksters and trickery 13, 15, 26–7, 45, 73, 78, 111–14
  see also under slaves: *servus callidus*
triumphs 34

umbra 15–16, 48
Umbria 9, 15–16
uxor dotata 31–2

venues
  Greek 18, 53–4
  Roman 17–18, 40, 43–4, 53–5, 91

Vergil 3, 49
violence, *see under* slaves and slavery
vortere 4, 14–15, 98, 106, 131 n.70

warfare and imperialism 4, 21, 33–4

Printed in the USA
CPSIA information can be obtained
at www.ICGtesting.com
LVHW050342300723
753750LV00002B/169